Awaken
MY Heart

"Reading and reflecting through this devotional, I was drawn closer to God's loving heart. I love how practical, deep, reflective, and thought-provoking this devotional is. Emily Wilson Hussem is a wonderful role model and through this book will awaken the hearts of women to the love of Christ."

Fr. Rob Galea
Musician, singer-songwriter, and author of *Breakthrough*

"In *Awaken My Heart*, Emily Wilson Hussem touches upon our desperation to be seen, heard, and loved. She answers back with the only answer that could satisfy such a desire: God alone. In a world full of negativity, this book will remind you that life is beautiful, joy awaits, and God will never leave you. Every human being needs this book."

Leah Darrow
Catholic speaker, podcaster, and
author of *The Other Side of Beauty*

"I want every woman to read this book. No matter your age or season of life, Emily Wilson Hussem's voice is full of encouragement, compassion, wisdom, and truth. She speaks right to your heart. Her personal stories bring scripture and faith in Jesus to life. *Awaken My Heart* truly does what it promises: it awakens the heart of every woman fortunate enough to read it."

Beth Davis
Director of Ministry Advancement
Blessed Is She

"Deep interior growth takes healing, time, and reflection—a difficult task to complete on our own. Through personal stories, tremendous practical insights, and countless tips for refocusing and putting our Lord at the center of our lives, Emily Wilson Hussem

offers her hand as a sister in Christ and walks with us, leaving a profound and powerful impression on us all. What a gift!"

Sarah Swafford
Catholic speaker and author of *Emotional Virtue*

"What a gift we have in Emily Wilson Hussem, an author who speaks to the heart of young women with such great clarity, truth, and love, and who now has written *Awaken My Heart* to journey with them for the whole year. Every young woman who reads this book will be reminded of the glory of who they are and *whose* they are."

Jackie Francois Angel
Speaker, songwriter, and author of *Pray, Decide, and Don't Worry*

Awaken MY Heart

52 Weeks of Giving Thanks and Loving Abundantly

A YEARLY DEVOTIONAL FOR WOMEN

EMILY WILSON HUSSEM

Ave Maria Press AVE Notre Dame, Indiana

© 2020 by Emily Wilson Hussem

Founded in 1865, Ave Maria Press is a ministry of the United States Province of Holy Cross.

www.avemariapress.com

Paperback: ISBN-13 978-1-64680-021-6

E-book: ISBN-13 978-1-64680-022-3

Cover image © Katerina Osa/Creative Market.

Cover and text design by Brianna Dombo.

Printed and bound in the United States of America.

Library of Congress Cataloging-in-Publication Data
Names: Wilson Hussem, Emily, author.
Title: Awaken my heart : 52 weeks of giving thanks and loving abundantly : a yearly devotional for women / Emily Wilson Hussem.
Description: Notre Dame, Indiana : Ave Maria Press, 2020. | Summary: "Emily Wilson Hussem invites readers on a year-long, transformational journey to noticing God, practicing gratitude, and serving others. These fifty-two reflections will help readers find freedom from the frenzy of tasks and accomplishments and discover the special joy of God's quiet, loving presence"-- Provided by publisher.
Identifiers: LCCN 2020024585 (print) | LCCN 2020024586 (ebook) | ISBN 9781646800216 (paperback) | ISBN 9781646800223 (ebook)
Subjects: LCSH: Christian women--Religious life--Meditations. | Christian women--Prayers and devotions.
Classification: LCC BV4527 .W5546 2020 (print) | LCC BV4527 (ebook) | DDC 242/.643--dc23
LC record available at https://lccn.loc.gov/2020024585
LC ebook record available at https://lccn.loc.gov/2020024586

For my nana,

a beautiful soul who knew what
it meant to live with a heart
awakened to the glory of God.

Contents

Acknowledgments

Mom and Dad, thank you
for the gift of faith.

Daniël, thank you
for the gift of your joy.

Jesus, thank you for everything.

Introduction

I am sitting on a plane that just took off from Seattle. The sun is sinking behind the horizon, and the sky shows every possible shade of orange, purple, and pink. Below me are snowcapped mountains, and the majesty of it all takes my breath away. I steal the moment to look and breathe in wonder at this awesome sight. Seldom do I find myself poised to pause and be present to my surroundings. It is rare that I stop and deeply appreciate the majesty of God.

As a new mom, I find that my life is pure pandemonium. I usually feel as if I'm being swept away by a chaotic chain of events that requires me to juggle a million balls at once—or perhaps not balls, but flaming torches. I used to think life would slow down after I graduated from college, or started my first job, or finished planning my wedding, or started a family. But the relentless pace of life keeps charging on, and most days I struggle to keep up. I struggle to carve out time for honest, dedicated, intimate prayer with God. I try to work from home while also being a stay-at-home mom, writing while the baby naps and tending to laundry, cooking, and errands while my husband is away at his full-time job. I often feel as if, instead of doing an excellent job at any one thing, I am doing a mediocre job of everything, and my mind and body are utterly exhausted from maintaining this pace.

Can you relate? Maybe you're in college, and you feel as if your classes, social life, internship, and career planning demand every ounce of your mental and physical resources. Or maybe you have four more children than I do, and you chuckle at the prospect of a woman who thinks that life with one child is chaotic. Perhaps you have a burgeoning career, and your job has you so spent at the end of the day that all you want to do when you get home is microwave a frozen dinner and go straight to bed.

Allow me to tell you a story. I heard this story from a Carmelite nun named Sr. Faustina. Though not original to me, this story is the central message of the book you are holding in your hands.

A woman was experiencing a particularly difficult season of life as the stresses of work, children, finances, and family left her feeling as if she was constantly in over her head. She lamented to her husband nightly about the lack of joy and peace in her everyday life. So, one day after work, the husband decided to bring home a bouquet of flowers for her.

He arranged the flowers in a vase and placed them lovingly on the dining room table to surprise her. When she got home, she was so absorbed in thinking about all she needed to prepare for the children for the next day, and was so stressed by a conversation she had had with a difficult coworker that day, that she passed by the table several times without even noticing the flowers. Instead, she finished her daily tasks and went right to bed.

Can you imagine the husband's sorrow as he thought, *She didn't see them?*

Now let's imagine for a moment that God is working similarly in our lives. He leaves flowers for us every day. He wants to surprise us with his unending love. Sadly, though, we often don't pay attention. We are either too consumed by the stress of our lives or so busy looking at everyone else's flowers that we do not even notice the brilliant bouquet before us. Chaos distracts us. To-do lists prevent us from noticing. And to top it all off, we have a list of

excuses as to why we don't have time to pray and cultivate a true, deep connection with God. Yet we know in our hearts that our prayer life is the lifeblood of our faith.

We are immersed in a culture of hustle, which tells us we can only succeed and be happy by exerting ourselves at maximum capacity. Hustle culture does not sleep. It does not stop to notice sunsets and springtime blossoms. It does not pause to experience God. Hustle culture is waking up on the weekend and making spreadsheets, not pancakes. We feel as if we have to keep doing, doing, doing. But we're running on empty, and our hearts are hurting.

Hustle culture never stops to sleep, but I have come to see that it has put many of our hearts to sleep. We go through the motions as though our eyes are closed, and our hearts are losing an awareness of the gift of life, the miracles of God, the beauty of the soul in front of us. As I began to pray about this book, I was stirred to a realization that sometimes I am sleepwalking through life. I am physically in motion, but my heart is asleep to the majesty of God's presence in my life and in the world. I felt God call me to an awakening. And that's what I hope this book can be for you: an awakening to the glory of God.

In this book, we're going to journey together through an entire year as we learn how to live life present to the bountiful gifts God provides. I want your heart to be awakened to him who adores you more than you can imagine. But *how* does he love? Last time I checked, he wasn't slipping love notes in my journal or cleaning the kitchen for me. No. He works in quieter, more beautiful ways. He leaves bouquets of blessings on every surface of our lives, and it's up to us to notice.

What is your bouquet? It is your friends, your family, your education, your community, the big blessings, and the little blessings—your bouquet is all of the beauty of your life, even the beauty you have not taken the time to notice. I invite you to allow the Lord

to surprise you this year. Take a wide-angle lens to your life and zoom out.

Each week of this year, we will focus on a different area where your heart may need awakening. Each reflection is designed to draw you deeper into the heart of God by learning to love Jesus, others, and yourself more fully. You can choose which day to make your devotional day—my recommendation is Sunday, the day of rest, and I hope that this book is an avenue for just that. But if your day off work is Wednesday, and that is when you have the most time for reflection and prayer, let your devotional day be Wednesday. This is a flexible journey between you and your Maker, and you get to decide together how that will look.

Little transformation is possible if we are unwilling to look honestly into our hearts. Many of the weeks will encourage you to dig deep, and that takes time. It takes effort. It takes real thought and dedicated prayer. That is why I made these weekly reflections—so that you can lean into what God is asking you to think about for the week and let him do some molding and shaping that cannot happen in one day.

At the conclusion of each chapter, I've provided some "Soul Exercises," which will help you search your heart and soul for how the week's reflection applies to your daily life. Following the Soul Exercises, you'll find "Your Heart's Prayer This Week." To get the most out of this journey, plan to return to each chapter a few times during the week—perhaps reading the reflection on day one, then journaling through one exercise on day two, then another on day three, and so forth. Again, this is all at your own pace; there are no rules! I invite you to pray the prayer each day of that week, and also to feel free to create your own. My hope is that the prompts will assist you throughout this year of transformation, and that the prayer offers you a place to begin your conversation with Jesus.

We must stop. We must look. We must breathe in the glory of God around us. When we do, our hearts awaken to God's love. We wake up from our slumber to see him more clearly, hear him more distinctly, and know him more intimately in the love he has for us and the love for him that grows ever deeper in our hearts.

I invite you this year to pause with intention, to pay attention to God's work in your life, to love others abundantly, and to give thanks for every moment—all so that God can awaken your heart to his profound love for you.

Week 1

Receive His Peace

Sometimes we mix up the words *peace* and *order*. They are not interchangeable. They are not equal. But sometimes we fall into believing that they are one and the same.

Often we mistakenly believe that to have peace in our hearts, everything has to be going well. Everyone has to be getting along, all of our desires must be fulfilled, and all the ducks must be in a row. As the world sees it, peace is a result of everyone being happy and everything going smoothly. But Jesus gives a peace that makes no sense to the world: "Then the peace of God that surpasses all understanding will guard your hearts and minds in Christ Jesus" (Phil 4:7).

Several years ago, I ran across a video online of a few dozen people singing songs of praise to the Lord. The scene was very moving and the singing was beautiful, but the situation in which the singers were giving God glory was unexpected. These people were gathered around cots in a stadium that was being used as a shelter during a hurricane. These people had been evacuated from their houses and were in danger of losing loved ones and their homes, yet their song was filled with peace. They were praising God in the middle of disaster, even though nothing about the situation was ideal. Evidence of your reliance on the Lord is feeling his peace even in the midst of terrible storms, both literally and figuratively.

How does this happen? How can we find peace even when nothing is going right? By turning our gaze and our hearts to him who is Peace, and uttering the simplest of prayers: *Jesus, be my peace.*

This prayer was my only recourse as I approached the birth of my son, Zion. I was blessed that my C-section was not an emergency—neither Zion nor I was in immediate danger, but my body had progressed as far as it would go, and we had run out of options for a safe delivery. It was interesting to experience because the moment the doctor decided to do a C-section, everyone went into action. They quickly started moving the bed and preparing medical

equipment; things became quite chaotic. It was organized chaos, but chaos nonetheless. Our birthing class did not cover C-sections in detail, so every moment of the process was totally unanticipated. Several nurses were readying me and my body to get the baby out, while the doctor was suited up and my husband, Daniël, prepared. There was no peace in this process as the world defines it.

And yet, in the midst of it all, I have never felt more peace. I have never felt less anxious. I have never felt such a lack of worry or trouble in my life than in that room, in that moment, on that day.

Why? Because I had unshakable confidence and peace in Christ himself.

God was showing me that even in the middle of mayhem, when you cling to Christ, you can find a wellspring of peace that does not make any "sense." I was speechless at the peace I felt. The Lord told us that we would not understand how we could have such peace (Phil 4:7); it is the result of anchoring our hearts in him in all things, as we turn our gaze and heart to him each day.

Your life may be chaos. Maybe you have had weeks, or months, or even years of chaos. If that is the case, I share this prayer with you to hold on to for the rest of your life: *Jesus, be my peace.*

This week I invite you to find peace right here, right now, even if things are all out of order. Peace doesn't depend on the messiness of your current moment; it's about finding yourself in the heart of God to say, no matter what is happening in my life today, God is my refuge. He is my rock. He makes all things work together for the good of those who love him (Rom 8:28). He is my fortress and my shield, and I find peace in him—not the peace that comes and goes with my circumstances, but a peace that lasts forever.

SOUL EXERCISES

1. Where do you need Christ to bring his peace into your life right now?
2. Philippians 4:7 speaks of the peace of Christ that surpasses all understanding—the kind of peace that does not make sense to our human minds. Has there been a time in your life when you felt unexplainable peace, even in the midst of a great struggle? Reflect on this time and let it teach you about the peace Christ always wants to give you.

YOUR HEART'S PRAYER THIS WEEK

Jesus, you are the Prince of Peace. Thank you for providing the peace that only you can give in every circumstance of my life. Thank you for being my refuge in the chaos of life, in the uncertainties of my journey, and on my brightest days. Help me to rest, always, in the serenity of your heart and your presence. Jesus, be my peace for the rest of my days. Amen.

Week 2

Seek Him

We can glean many spiritual lessons from the well-known parable of the prodigal son. As a cradle Catholic, I have heard numerous reflections on this parable throughout my life of faith. Most explanations highlight our propensity to run from God in our sin and his willingness to accept us with love when we come to our senses, repent, and come back home to his loving and merciful arms.

I recently heard a new perspective on this parable that helped me better understand the depth of commitment that God is asking of me. First, I want to share a portion of the scripture with you to take and reflect on throughout this week. The prodigal son has returned home, and his older brother gets upset:

> He became angry, and when he refused to enter the house, his father came out and pleaded with him. He said to his father in reply, "Look, all these years I served you and not once did I disobey your orders; yet you never gave me even a young goat to feast on with my friends. But when your son returns who swallowed up your property with prostitutes, for him you slaughter the fattened calf." He said to him, "My son, you are here with me always; everything I have is yours." (Lk 15:28–31)

Both sons wanted what the father could give more than they wanted the father. The first son wanted his inheritance *right then* (Lk 15:12), placing material goods over his current relationship with his father. The older brother wanted a substantial gift, such as a goat, that he could share with his friends, again caring more about his father's possessions than his father. Neither son focused on spending time with his father—to love him, to be in his company as his son. They prioritized earthly possessions over the father-son relationship.

We can fall into the same trap with God: we seek what God can give us rather than God himself. This is what the older son

expressed that he desired—a reward, a goat to share with his friends, for his faithfulness to his father.

Have you ever desired a reward for your faithfulness? I have.

I have sought rewards from the Lord for my fidelity to him and have expected his good favor for loving him. I have been frustrated on the hard road of faith when I have seen women who I know have not been following Christ appear to receive more blessings in life than me (perhaps you know how this feels). Additionally, there have been times and seasons when I have constantly presented to the Lord a list of the things I'd like him to do rather than simply sat in his presence to say over and over, *Lord, I love you.*

And that's it. Not . . . Lord, I love you, and *can you give me this?* Not . . . Lord, I love you, and *can you do this for me?*

These are not *bad* prayers, but we have to be careful of running toward God while looking over his shoulder to see what he is going to give us—a husband, a baby, a house, a better job, a cure, a financial blessing.

Do you follow God and try to remain faithful to his (sometimes difficult) commandments because of *who he is* or because of *what he can do?* This week, I invite you to ponder this question as you take a hard look at your motives in following Jesus, and at your prayer life. How have you been praying lately? Are you crying out to God over what he has not given you, or are you stopping to give him glory and gratitude simply for who he is?

When we look at the parable of the prodigal son, we must pause to ask ourselves, *Am I seeking a Person or a prize?*

Let us seek the Lord because we love him—not because of what he does or what he gives, but because of who he is.

SOUL EXERCISES

1. Have you ever tried to draw close to God in hopes that he would give you a desire of your heart? What was that desire? Did it become an idol in your life, or is it currently an idol in your life? Pray with the Lord about this desire, asking him to help you surrender it to him.

2. Have you ever been frustrated because those around you who do not follow God seem to be rewarded more in life than you? Have an honest conversation with God about that, and be open to listening to what he has to say.

YOUR HEART'S PRAYER THIS WEEK

Jesus, I want to seek you above all else. Help me to relinquish my desire for reward, recognition, or a prize for my faithfulness. Grant me a desire to know you more, to love you more, to run toward you with open arms—not looking over your shoulder, but looking only at you, my greatest love. Thank you for all that you are. You are more than enough for me. Awaken my heart to a greater desire for *you*. Amen.

Week 3

Let Him Soften Your Heart

But to you who hear I say,
love your enemies, do good to
those who hate you, bless those
who curse you, pray for those who
mistreat you.
—Luke 6:27–28

What does it mean to have an enemy? You and I are not going to war. There is no enemy attack about to take place—but in my life, I consider enemies to be the people who have hurt me badly, the people who make fun of my faith, the people who try purposefully to make my life miserable. Enemies like these can be anywhere—at school, in the workplace, even in our family.

None of Jesus' teachings are easy, but this is one of the hardest ones: Do good to those who hate you. We were told countless times as children that *hate* is a very strong word that we should never use. Extending forgiveness to people who are our enemies, who hate us, who mistreat us, seems like enough, doesn't it? But in Luke 6:27–28, Jesus asks us to go a step further. He *commands* us to take action beyond forgiveness; he doesn't say, "You probably should. Maybe it would be a good idea." He gives imperative commands . . .

Love. Do good. Bless. Pray.

I struggle greatly with adhering to this command. The last thing I want to do is do good to those who hate me and pray for the people who have mistreated me. Forgiveness can be difficult enough for our human hearts. It often takes much reflection, surrender, and prayer to come to forgive people who have mistreated us.

But that step beyond forgiveness into love, into prayer, into blessing those people, is an act of mercy. Loving your enemies is an act of mercy. And Matthew 5:7 is clear about those who show mercy to others: "Blessed are the merciful, for they will be shown mercy." Mercy is something that is undeserved. It is something we receive from Christ every day of our lives out of the love in his heart, and he asks us to love in the exact same way.

Have you ever taken intentional time to pray for the people in your life who you dislike so much that you feel repulsed by the thought of praying for them? A few years ago, I went through an extremely hard situation with a friend who betrayed me. It was very ugly for many reasons, and a few months after our big fallout I decided I had to begin praying for this person. I didn't want to,

but I decided to try. Praying intentionally for this person felt like having soap in my mouth at the start. The words came bitterly out of my mouth as I tried to take the first step in following this command of Christ. But I kept at it. I did it again and again. And I don't know how my prayers affected that person, but I know how they affected me. They gave me new eyes to see. Christ gave me the eyes to see this person as he sees them—hurting badly from deep wounds and desperately needing peace. As I prayed more, it got easier, and my heart softened, thanks be to God. Our God is in the business of softening hearts.

This week I invite you to pray deeply through this verse: "But to you who hear I say, love your enemies, do good to those who hate you, bless those who curse you, pray for those who mistreat you" (Lk 6:27–28). What does loving your enemies look like for you? Consider trying one or both of these suggestions this week:

- ❤ Write down all your feelings about a situation in which someone hurt you, and conclude with a prayer for that person.
- ❤ Ask God to give you the strength and grace to pray for the person who hurt you, or to teach you how to live out Luke 6:27–28 in your life.

You can focus on a different person each day of this week, or maybe you need to concentrate your efforts of prayer on one situation, one person, one deep hurt. Whichever the case is for you, Christ is present as you follow his command. He knows that it is not easy. He knows that it doesn't come naturally. Take one small step and let him guide you into the next one and the one after that with love, peace, and mercy.

SOUL EXERCISES

1. Which situations and people come to mind when Jesus talks about praying for our enemies? Who is he asking you to pray for this week and beyond?
2. Have you ever prayed for someone who hurt you deeply? If yes, what kind of freedom or consolation did you find in doing so?

YOUR HEART'S PRAYER THIS WEEK

Jesus, it is not easy to follow your command to love my enemies, to do good to those who have hurt me deeply. I cannot do it on my own! Grant me the grace to take that first small step of calling to mind those you want me to pray for, and to lift them up to you. Help me to let go of any resentment and grudges I am consciously or unconsciously holding on to, so that, ultimately, I can find the peace you long for me to live in. This week, I choose to love my enemies with courage—help me to do just that. Amen.

**Week
4**

Uproot Jealousy

One night I was on the treadmill at the gym, glancing around at the shows on the many giant screens spread out in front of me. I watched a commercial for Anthony Bourdain's *Parts Unknown* TV show and thought very vividly to myself, *Wow, his life is so exciting. I wish my life was that thrilling—traveling all over the world, meeting all kinds of people. Sheesh, I would love that.* Tragically, Bourdain died by suicide just two weeks after that visit to the gym. I was stunned when I read the news online, remembering my envy of his fantastic and exciting life just a couple of weeks prior.

Most of our jealousy in our social media–saturated culture stems from what we perceive people's lives to be. We're not jealous of their actual lives—we're jealous of their highlight reel, because we see our own highlight *and* lowlight reel every single day. So often we are jealous only of what we perceive someone to be—a classmate who has a ton of accolades and success on the outside but who is crumbling on the inside, a mom-friend who seems to have it all together but is actually suffering, this man on a TV show who was traveling to exotic places but struggling silently with depression.

Jealousy is sneaky. It can overtake our thoughts and even creep into our motives. When jealousy is allowed to fester and goes unchecked in our hearts, it develops into bitterness or resentment—the tools the enemy has used since the beginning of time to diminish our belief in the goodness of God. And bitterness that is allowed to grow deep roots within us has the power to affect our faith in tremendously negative ways.

Jealousy can play a huge role in our experiences as women, causing us to lose focus on what God is doing and speaking into our own lives. We spend our days looking around to see what he is doing in the lives of the women around us, whether in person or online, asking, "What does she have going on in her life, what is God doing for her, what blessings is she receiving that I am not?" Our necks sometimes seem permanently turned to the side as we look at the lives of others rather than the life before us. We see other

women who have what we want—a great job, a sweet husband, children, a prettier or cleaner house, a bigger following, a family that looks like they enjoy spending time together—and we look longingly, sometimes with envy, sometimes with bitterness, and we say, "I want her life, Lord."

When God doesn't grant prayers or wishes like these, we let it affect our relationship with him. Rather than affirming that he is good, we believe he is withholding. Even as he tries to make his presence known to us, we are fast asleep to the reality of his presence and his movement. We begin to say things to the Lord along the lines of, "Well, Lord, you must love her more. If you loved me as much as you love her, you would give me those things, too." And when we begin to measure God's love for us according to what he has or has not done for us, we get into very dangerous territory. When our faith in God is rooted in what he gives or doesn't give, it will come and go. Faith is a journey, certainly, and there are twists and turns all along the path, but if I cannot praise God both in desolation and in consolation, in the pruning and in the harvest, when he gives and when he takes away, then my faith will be a constant roller coaster of "You are so good, Lord!" when everything is going my way, and "God, you must not love me!" when things are not.

If my faith is rooted in who God is, rather than in what he gives or doesn't give, I can say, "You are good!" when God is bestowing good things upon me. And when things are not going my way, in seasons and years of waiting or suffering, I can still say, "Yes, Lord, even in this, you are good."

God's goodness does not depend on the circumstances of my life. And his goodness does not depend on what he gives to others but not to me. His goodness stands in the midst of it all.

This week I invite you to think about what part jealousy plays in your life. If we want to live in union with God, we must do the heart work necessary to cease from turning our head side to side to look at everyone else's blessings, to cease from resenting God for

apparently favoring some of his children over others. I invite you to renew your resolve this week to look forward at all times, consumed by the love of God in good times and in bad. Because the reality of our lives is this: Jesus died a horrific death out of infinite love for each and every one of us on the Cross, and he gives an equal outpouring of his love to each of us. If that is not enough for us to spend our lives in joyful gratitude rather than in bitter jealousy, nothing ever will be.

SOUL EXERCISES

1. Upon honest reflection, would you consider yourself a jealous person? Have you had seasons when you struggle more with this sin than others? Why?
2. What qualities and circumstances are you most envious of when you look around? How can you change your outlook to see the beauty before you and to give thanks to God for everything he is doing in your life?

YOUR HEART'S PRAYER THIS WEEK

Jesus, I do not wish to live my life as a jealous person. I ask you, on this journey, to root out the sin of jealousy from my heart and from my life. Remove the scales from my eyes so that I may see the beauty of the life you have given me, the gifts you have bestowed on me, and your heart's love for me. Help me to keep my gaze fixed forward, walking in faith as a woman who celebrates and does not tear down, a woman always found singing the praises of God in gratitude and joy. Amen.

Week
5

Pray the Litany for Healing of Body Image

This week we will focus on loving our bodies exactly as God created them. I've written a Litany for Healing of Body Image, which is tailored to our unique struggle as women to accept and appreciate our bodies. A litany is a poetic form of prayer made of a series of short phrases followed by the same response. You may be familiar with the Litany of Humility or the Litany of Trust. This litany is similar in format, but offers to the Lord the entirety of your body image as a woman—both the positive and negative feelings, and the actions that you have taken or neglected, throughout your journey of learning to love the body God gave you. There are four movements to this litany, each with a statement and prayer response at the end.

Whether you are currently in a season where you struggle deeply with insecurity about your body, or in a season where you feel deep appreciation for the body you live in, God gave me this prayer for you. I hope that you will use it for many years to come to give praise and thanks to God for the beautiful creation that is your body, the place where God dwells. If you can, pray this litany every day this week. See how it transforms your relationship with your body.

How magnificently God created each one of us! Let us pray . . .

That I would treat my body with love and care . . .
  Jesus, give me the grace.

That I would choose food that nourishes and sustains me . . .
  Jesus, give me the grace.

That I would come to realize the care you took in crafting me . . .
  Jesus, give me the grace.

That I would come to accept the parts of my body I wish you had made differently . . .
  Jesus, give me the grace.

That I would come to love the parts of my body I wish you had made differently . . .
  Jesus, give me the grace.

For the energy to exercise as regularly as possible at this time in my life . . .
> *Jesus, give me the grace.*

For the discipline to tend to my health rather than neglect it . . .
> *Jesus, give me the grace.*

For peace in believing that you did not make any mistakes when you made me . . .
> *Jesus, give me the grace.*

For acceptance of the way my cultural heritage is reflected in my body . . .
> *Jesus, give me the grace.*

For serenity in knowing my body is supposed to be different than the bodies of my friends . . .
> *Jesus, give me the grace.*

For the courage to look away from unrealistic examples of beauty and look to you instead . . .
> *Jesus, give me the grace.*

For mothers: For the wisdom to see that my body grew a life and is not supposed to look like it did before my child was born . . .
> *Jesus, give me the grace.*

From any tendency to hate the way you made me . . .
> *deliver me, Jesus.*

From the pressure to fit my body into a certain mold . . .

deliver me, Jesus.

From the fear that my physical appearance makes me unlovable . . .
deliver me, Jesus.

From the temptation to skip meals . . .
deliver me, Jesus.

From the belief that more attractive women are better than me . . .
deliver me, Jesus.

From the desire to artificially alter my appearance . . .
deliver me, Jesus.

From the temptation to place my identity in my appearance . . .
deliver me, Jesus.

From the fear that my appearance will keep me from achieving my dreams . . .
deliver me, Jesus.

From the temptation to believe that as a woman I am defined by my appearance . . .
deliver me, Jesus.

For the times I have not treated my body like the sacred temple it is . . .
forgive me, Jesus.

For the times I have looked in the mirror and hated your creation . . .

forgive me, Jesus.

For the times I have fallen into gluttony . . .
  forgive me, Jesus.

For the times I have turned to food instead of turning to
  you . . .
  forgive me, Jesus.

For the times I have exercised excessively rather than in a
  healthy way . . .
  forgive me, Jesus.

For the times I have been angry with you for the way you
  crafted other women . . .
  forgive me, Jesus.

For the times I have put other women down because I am
  jealous of their beauty . . .
  forgive me, Jesus.

For the times I have let jealousy of other women affect my
  love for you . . .
  forgive me, Jesus.

For the eyes you gave me . . .
  Jesus, I praise you.

For the hands you gave me . . .
  Jesus, I praise you.

For the hips you gave me . . .
  Jesus, I praise you.

For the heart you gave me . . .
  Jesus, I praise you.

For the bone structure you gave me . . .
  Jesus, I praise you.

For the chest you gave me . . .
  Jesus, I praise you.

For the legs you gave me . . .
  Jesus, I praise you.

For the nose you gave me . . .
  Jesus, I praise you.

For the hair you gave me . . .
  Jesus, I praise you.

For the ways my body becomes more womanly over time . . .
  Jesus, I praise you.

For making me unique and unrepeatable in your image and
likeness . . .
  *Jesus, I praise you and thank you, today, tomorrow,
  and forever.*

Amen.

SOUL EXERCISES

1. Which lines of the litany speak to your heart? Take an inventory of your struggles with body image. What have your past challenges been, and what do you wrestle with today?
2. As you pray this litany this week, imagine Jesus, in his goodness and tenderness, standing before you holding your hands. Place yourself in the scene with him and be open to his love and his responses as you pray.

YOUR HEART'S PRAYER THIS WEEK

Pray at least one section of the Litany for Healing of Body Image every day, building up to the whole prayer. Or, if you feel that a certain section touches on an area of your life that needs healing and restoration, pray that section every day. However you approach the litany this week, pray this short line as often as possible: *Jesus, thank you for creating me in your image and likeness.*

Week
6

Become
Childlike

Jesus said, "Let the children
come to me, and do not prevent
them; for the kingdom of heaven
belongs to such as these."
—Matthew 19:14

One day when I was four years old, while my family was sitting around the dinner table, I stood up on my chair and exclaimed out of the blue, "I'm full of life!" as I threw my arms into the air. It's a story my mom and dad tell often. My parents have used that story to describe me many times—I do love life, and I have a zest for soaking it all in.

All small children do.

They have a penchant for curiosity; they have a wonder and awe. Most children are willing to make friends with a stranger at the drop of a hat. Their hearts are free, and for one reason or another, when we grow up, that freedom is harder and harder to find.

Once when Daniël and I were eating outdoors at a pizza restaurant in Laguna Beach, we found ourselves delighting in the joy of a little boy who was jumping around being silly at the crosswalk. His dad was close by and apologized to us. The boy continued to hop around gleefully, and the dad continued to apologize for his son's spirited behavior.

"It's fine! We don't mind!" I said to him happily each time he spoke to us. But what I really wanted to say by his third apology was this: *"Sir, there is absolutely no need to apologize. If there is anything this world needs, it is the vibrancy your son brings to it . . . the unhindered joy that causes him to hop around, singing silly songs and using his imagination with glee. We all need it. Let him be joyful, and do not be concerned about what anyone thinks of it—because anyone who is annoyed by it needs to take a page out of your son's book of joy."*

I wish I had. It saddened me that this man felt the need to apologize, but I know why he did: many people today are annoyed by children, and they make this very clear to parents. Children can certainly be exasperating when they screech or cry or throw tantrums, but far more often we see children exhibit a joyful spirit and an uninhibited authenticity that allows them to be fully and deeply themselves. They have so much to teach us.

I once visited my sister Gracie at the day camp where she worked during the summer. Tons of lively little children were bouncing around on the beach. One little girl came up to me and sweetly said, "Hi! I'm Phoebe! Do you want to be my friend?" She looked at me with her hopeful and curious blue eyes, freckles sprinkled across her nose and cheeks. She did not wait to hear my response, but enthusiastically grabbed my hand and said, "Come with me!"

And just like that, in an instant, I was welcomed. I was greeted in her world with joy and a big smile. In just a few seconds she had shown me that she accepted me. Reflecting on this later, I wondered, *How often do I as a woman express my acceptance of others in the way that children do so easily? How often does a new woman come into a space where I belong and I greet her with love and joy and an invitation, rather than a cold shoulder or unwelcoming glance?* Phoebe shared a part of her tiny heart with me in that brief moment—the part that feels totally free to befriend others and sing joy into their hearts. As an innocent five-year-old, she does not have stacks of rejection memories from when her invitation to friendship was declined or when she was made to feel unwelcome by other girls. Her unscathed heart allows her to extend her hand. Meanwhile, we grown-ups let our wounded hearts discourage us from putting ourselves out there.

This week is about noticing the spirit and joy of children and letting their example teach us. You don't have to go out of your way. In fact, as I write this, sitting at a table in a coffee shop, a tiny girl stands next to me holding a gift card and joyfully plays it like a harmonica. And I think to myself . . . *I want to be more like her.* Less reserved, more myself. Less rigid, more imaginative. On the other side of the café, another girl sips a little drink and clutches a large plush carrot. I am not sure why she has this carrot with her, but she is completely oblivious to any judgy onlookers. I want to be free like her, to care less about what people think.

Watch the children in your life this week. You'll see them every-where, and their spirit and joy, I am certain, will be on display for you to delight in and learn from.

What can they teach you? In what ways do you need to get back to being more like a child? Children know how to live awake and alive in the grandeur of God. Let us pay quiet and careful attention to their example so we can let those beautiful parts of our carefree spirit that have faded away come back to life.

SOUL EXERCISE

Recall a memory from when you were a small girl who felt truly wild and free in the unique way children do. If you can't remember right away, invite the Holy Spirit to show you. Breathe deeply and try to relive in your heart that moment from your childhood. What feelings bubble up?

YOUR HEART'S PRAYER
THIS WEEK

Jesus, I have lost so much of the joy and freedom I had when I was a little girl. Please awaken that joy in my heart and in my soul. Help me to obey your command to become like a little child so that my faith may increase tenfold. Help me to focus on the spirit and joy of the children in my life this week. May I learn from their example of exuberance and love for you. Amen.

Week
7

Find Your Own Calcutta

One of the most inspiring stories I have ever heard is the story of Katie Davis, a young woman who moved to Uganda when she was eighteen years old. She visited the country on a high school trip and then felt called by God to move there to serve the poor immediately after graduation. A few years later she adopted thirteen young women, and many years after that she began a school to provide education for thousands of Ugandan children. Her story reflects an astounding love for the Lord and his people and a stunning obedience to God's call to love the poor. (If you want to learn more about Katie's work, check out Amazima Ministries online.) It is easy to look at Katie's life and think, *Wow, I'll never be able to go to those lengths to serve the Lord,* or, *She is doing a way better job serving God than I am.*

It is easy to believe that a missionary in a foreign country is somehow more obedient to the Lord, is sacrificing more, or is simply a better follower of Jesus than we are. The nature of the call God has placed on their life and all that they do to serve him give rise to that belief. But here is the truth that the Lord wants us to know: We each have our own Calcutta.

We might not ever become as well-known as Katie or Mother Teresa of Calcutta, the modern-day saint who spent most of her life serving the people in the slums of India, but that doesn't mean we aren't doing important work. Let's reflect on the words of Mother Teresa herself: "Stay where you are. Find your own Calcutta. Find the sick, the suffering, and the lonely right there where you are—in your own homes and in your own families, in your workplaces and in your schools. You can find Calcutta all over the world, if you have the eyes to see. Everywhere, wherever you go, you find people who are unwanted, unloved, uncared for, just rejected by society—completely forgotten, completely left alone."

God does not call all of us to serve his people in poor countries. The beautiful thing about your life and my life is that there are people right in front of us who may not look poor but who have a

poverty of heart that can only be remedied by someone introducing them to the love of Jesus Christ—and God has placed you or me in that person's path to do just that. It is God's call for each of us to find those most in need of love right before us.

What is your Calcutta? Perhaps it's the hospital where you work, or your classroom, your extended family, your office, or your home. Perhaps your Calcutta right now is one single person—whether that is a parent, a teen in your ministry, a coworker, your best friend, or someone else in need of great love. This kind of work can be done in so many different ways. For example, a middle-aged man at my church brings his mother with Alzheimer's disease to Mass every single day. I watch him guide her compassionately into the church, help her follow the liturgy, and assist her throughout the service. It's obvious—his mother is his Calcutta. At this moment, she is the sick and suffering person right before him.

When we reframe our vision as Mother Teresa said, there are Calcuttas all over the world. And as much as I want to be like Katie Davis, Uganda is not my Calcutta. Mine is the hearts of women all over the world—women who feel unwanted, unloved, uncared for, forgotten, and alone. My call is to bolster their hearts with the truth of the love of Christ—to meet them where they are and, by sharing in person and online, to make certain they know they are cared for and loved by a God who wants a deep relationship with them. When I was a high school teacher, my Calcutta was the hearts of the students who came to sit in my office and allowed me to guide them and journey with them. Now that I'm a mother, I have a small Calcutta in my home, too. Your Calcutta will not always be the same—mine has changed over time, and so will yours.

In the same way that Mother Teresa found people on the street in desperate need of love and attention, we have people in front of us every day who are in need of care—perhaps not physical care, but care of their hearts and souls. Your love for them matters. It is powerful. It gives glory to God, who wants his children loved by

us, his disciples, from Calcutta to Detroit to every city and home and community in the world.

Find your own Calcutta this week. And praise God for the opportunity to be his hands and feet to souls in need of his love, his mercy . . . but most simply, in need of him.

SOUL EXERCISES

1. Have you struggled with the feeling that you're not "doing enough" as a woman of faith? Look back on your spiritual journey and identify where you learned to compare God's call in your life to his call in the lives of others.
2. What is your Calcutta? Who in your life feels unwanted, forgotten, or alone?
3. Take some time to write about where your Calcutta has been in the past. Reflect on the ways God asked you to serve during that time, how faithfully you responded to that invitation, and how he may be asking you to serve now.

YOUR HEART'S PRAYER THIS WEEK

Jesus, I get discouraged when I feel as if I don't "do enough." Awaken my heart to my Calcutta, where you are calling me to serve the lost, the lonely, the poor, and the needy right before me. Give me the courage to love them as you do and the grace to serve exactly where you are calling me to serve, whether that is in a disadvantaged country or simply at home. Amen.

Week 8

Proclaim the Greatness of the Lord

Sometimes it can be easy to think, *Absolutely nothing is going my way, nothing at all.* And in the darkness of those days and nights, we can become consumed by the false idea that God has forgotten us and God doesn't care. Imagine if during these times of blue moods and depressive thoughts you could turn to a list of the blessings of your life. The list would be penned in your handwriting, and it would include items like:

- I have a roof over my head.
- I am in good health.
- I have a community of friends and mentors.
- My dog gave me a kiss today when I was feeling down.
- My child is healthy.
- My husband is faithful.

Do you think it would be easier to navigate those feelings of worthlessness and anxiety if you could easily recall how blessed you are? Certainly, we have to zoom out to see those blessings sometimes, especially when life has dealt us a tough hand or a hard day. But if you have a list—a gratitude list—of the great things our Lord has done for you, it might be easier to see how God is present, even in the midst of life's struggles. Yes, God does care. And no matter how difficult the season may be, life is full of blessings. Let's see Mary, the Mother of God, as our model here. She had a gratitude list of her own, which we can find in her Magnificat in the Gospel of Luke:

> And Mary said:
>
> "My soul proclaims the greatness of the Lord;
>   my spirit rejoices in God my savior.
> For he has looked upon his handmaid's lowliness;
>   behold, from now on will all ages call me blessed.
> The Mighty One has done great things for me,
>   and holy is his name." (Lk 1:46–49)

The Lord has done great things for me. This week, I want you to develop a list of those great things the Lord has done for you, and if you feel inspired, write your own Magnificat, trusting in God's generosity.

In Christ's first miracle, the wedding feast at Cana, the Lord shows that he not only gives, but gives in generosity and abundance. He pours out his love. But you and I live in a culture that shouts in our faces, *You need more.* Our minds are co-opted into thinking that we never have enough, and so we focus on what we think we *lack* rather than what we *have.* This spills over into our faith lives. We become fixated on what God *hasn't* given us. We can even trick ourselves into thinking that when Jesus said, "I came so that they might have life and have it more abundantly" (Jn 10:10), he meant an abundance of stuff, especially of what we have requested from God . . . lots of friends, children, a lucrative job or promotion, the perfect guy, the newest iPhone, money.

When we step back to look with clear vision, when we allow our hearts to be awakened to the truth, we can see that Jesus didn't say, "I came so that if you follow me you can get everything you want." He was telling us that we would have abundant life *in him.* We are called as followers of Christ to echo Mary's Magnificat in all we do—to proclaim the greatness of the Lord in our lives and attitudes.

Let's not become like the nine lepers in the Gospel of Luke who never returned: ten lepers are healed and only one comes back to give thanks (17:11–19). It is in giving thanks that we breathe in the bouquet before us. It is in giving thanks that we see the abundance of life that our negativity has blinded us to. It is in giving thanks that we gain new vision to see Christ at work.

The Christian life isn't about getting everything we want or about skating through life with no troubles. It is about looking for God in the midst of it all to say, "I am grateful," instead of "I want." When we shift our perspective toward unhindered gratitude, we echo Mary in our thoughts, words, and actions.

So, this week, I invite you to begin or revisit a gratitude list. I kept a gratitude journal when I taught at the high school, and it was life changing for me. I just took a little notebook and started writing down everything I was thankful for—from a great conversation with a friend to my shoes to the ability to work. I wrote out everything. And this week, I want you to do just that—to write, write, write. List off all the beauty of your life on paper and see a physical representation of all that God is, and praise him for it. Let it propel you into a song of thanksgiving, praise hands lifted to the sky, returning to him as the one leper did to say, *Thank you.*

SOUL EXERCISES

1. Is there an area in your life where you are buying into the cultural lie that you always need more? What is causing you to believe this?
2. Start that list: "I am grateful for . . ." One line at a time, give thanks to God for it all.

YOUR HEART'S PRAYER THIS WEEK

Jesus, you have done great things for me. Forgive me for all the times I've been bitterly ungrateful. Awaken my heart to celebrate all that you have done, all that you are doing, and all that you will do. Help me live a life that reflects my gratitude for who you are and who you will always be. I lift my hands to you today and with my whole heart say, "Thank you." Amen.

Week
9

Be Not
Afraid

In the scriptures, Jesus reminds us to "be not afraid" three hundred and sixty-five times—one time for each day of the year. It is a powerful statement that Jesus proclaims to many different people in the New Testament. It is a statement that people can get behind and say very easily. But this is one of the things in life that, for me, is much easier said than done.

For years, I have asked myself, *How do I just . . . not be afraid? How do I suddenly let go of my worries when someone tells me to?* I have experienced different fears in different seasons, and in many moments of my life fear has controlled me, consumed my days, and motivated my decisions. One such time was during my engagement to be married. I experienced deep fears about marriage that frequently kept me up at night. I had seen many beautiful examples of marriage throughout my life, but numerous people talked about how hard the first year of marriage would be. I heard it over and over again— "The first year of marriage is *so* hard!"—but no one would elaborate on what that meant, causing me a lot of fear. I wondered, would Daniël and I end up fighting all the time and hating each other as everyone seemed to imply we would? I heard of old friends getting divorced after relatively short marriages and wondered about the hardships marriage would bring for us. I felt God calling me to marry my husband but was terrified by what that might entail. I struggled to overcome those fears but eventually did with much prayer and guidance, and I am so glad I did!

When I operate out of fear, I am, in essence, telling the Lord that I don't believe him when he says he can be trusted in all things—when he says in scripture that I may not understand his ways but that his ways are good and trustworthy.

The scripture that resonates with me most in regard to fear is the story of the disciples in the boat with Jesus as he sleeps (Mk 4:38–40, RSV). All of a sudden, a storm comes upon the water, and the disciples are afraid (I would have been, too!). They wake Jesus up and ask him, "Do you not care?" Jesus immediately commands

the ocean to be still and then asks them a pointed question: "Why are you afraid?"

I imagine him looking them each in the eye, asking this question with love.

And as I reflect on this passage, I imagine Jesus standing with me in a boat, naming my biggest fears and asking me the very same question as I tremble, even in his presence. I imagine him taking me by the hands, looking me in the eyes, and saying, "Why are you afraid?"

It may be easy to identify or vocalize what we are afraid of—but we often do not take the time to reflect on *why* we are so afraid. So, this is a week to identify the what and the why, and to hand these aspects of our fears over to the Lord.

First, I ask you, what are you afraid of? What fears are you experiencing, the fears that take up space in your mind and heart, the fears that keep you up at night? Maybe they are in this list . . .

- Fear of failing.
- Fear of rejection.
- Fear of changing professions.
- Fear of being yourself.
- Fear of losing your friends if you talk about Jesus.
- Fear of being "undateable" if you save sex for marriage.
- Fear of what people think.
- Fear of being vulnerable.
- Fear of pregnancy or of having another baby.
- Fear of raising your children "wrong."
- Fear of never getting married.
- Fear of being left out.
- Fear of forging a path you are passionate about rather than the path others want for you.
- Fear of trying again after being rejected.
- Fear of the specific mission God has for you.

♥   Fear of the consequences of speaking the truth.
♥   Fear of the unknown.

Whatever your fears are, I invite you to picture yourself standing in that boat with the King of Kings, Jesus Christ himself, and allowing him to hold your hands in his and ask you with love and compassion, "Why are you afraid?"

Sometimes we have good reasons for our fears. Other times our fears are unfounded or irrational, and verbalizing why we are afraid can help expose that reality. To identify our fears and expose those delicate parts of our heart to Jesus is a very vulnerable move, but it makes way for the next and most beautiful step, which is active obedience to his command to "be not afraid." We must reveal those fearful parts of our heart to the Lord and ask him to turn our fear into faith. Christ wants to transform our worries into trust in his goodness. He wants you to stand with him in that boat, his almighty hands holding yours, and witness you handing over your fears so you can say to him in confidence, "Jesus, I trust in you!"

And so, I invite you to enter into an unpacking, a digging, a tender unfolding of your heart this week with the Lord, to take a careful look inside as you enter these three movements of transformation from fear into faith . . .

Jesus, these are my fears.
Jesus, this is why I am afraid.

Jesus, I surrender this fear to you

and ask you to turn it into faith
and trust in you.

SOUL EXERCISES

1. Take some time to enter into imaginative prayer
   with this scene this week:

   ♥ Close your eyes and imagine yourself
      standing in the boat with Christ. Imag-
      ine him asking you, "Why are you afraid?"
      Take your time to answer, and tell him
      your fears.

   ♥ Breathe deeply and pay attention to how
      Christ responds to the outpouring of
      your heart to him. How does he look?
      What does he say? Notice what his pres-
      ence in the midst of your fears does to
      your heart.

   ♥ Speak these verses from Psalm 107 aloud
      a few times as you breathe in and out:
      "In their distress they cried to the LORD,
      who brought them out of their peril; he
      hushed the storm to silence, the waves
      of the sea were stilled" (Ps 107:28–29).
      Spend some time in silence.

   ♥ Offer your fears to Christ and ask him
      to turn them into greater faith and trust
      in him.

2. As you imagine yourself standing with Jesus in
   the boat, what comes up in your heart? Does
   his presence in the midst of your fear change
   anything? Stand with him there, in your imaginative prayer, for as long as you need to. As you
   work through your fears with him this week, visit

that scene with him as many times as your heart needs to.

YOUR HEART'S PRAYER THIS WEEK

Jesus, I trust and believe that you did not create me for a life of fear. Help me to be a woman who chooses faith over fear in every facet of my life. Help me to let go of every one of my fears, knowing that as I stand before you, even in the midst of the storm, all will be well. I have nothing to fear because you are at my side, and you never leave. I surrender my fears to you and ask that you turn them into faith and trust. Amen.

Week 10

Let Him Heal You

For some of you, this will be the most difficult reflection on this entire journey. I do not write this reflection because I want you to feel pain, but out of obedience to God's prompting and desire for deep healing for each one of us. This week invites us to reflect on moments we wish had never happened and moments we wish we could forget. After reading that line, you may feel like skipping this reflection altogether. You surely *can* do so because this is your journey, but Christ wants healing for you and I encourage you not to. Cleaning wounds is a part of caring for them, and it can be terribly uncomfortable but necessary to the healing process. I pray for your heart very intentionally as I write this.

At some time in your life, in the midst of some event, you have felt abandoned or forgotten by God. It seems utterly impossible that an all-loving God was there with you. All logic tells you that in that moment he abandoned you. In that moment, he forgot you. In that moment, he didn't see that you needed him with you.

We have all had moments or seasons like this. We will all have more moments or seasons like this. And, as a woman of faith, in the question of abandonment by God, I have found that there is one place to go to find the answer to my questions . . . Matthew 27:46. As our Lord hung on the Cross near the end of his human life, "about three o'clock Jesus cried out in a loud voice, '*Eli, Eli, lema sabachthani?*' which means, 'My God, my God, why have you forsaken me?'" (Mt 27:46).

It is possible that you sobbed out the very same question Jesus Christ asked the Father in his final moments of deepest and most excruciating pain, "My God, my God, why have you forsaken me?" To feel forgotten, forsaken, abandoned by God—Jesus knew this pain very well.

You remember your own moments. The moment you made a choice that you knew you would regret for the rest of your life. The moment the doctor spoke the diagnosis out loud. The moment someone you love died or took their own life, and your world was

rearranged forever. The moment someone betrayed your trust deeply. The moment someone spoke a sentence to you that altered the course of your life forever. The moment your parents told you they were getting divorced. There are many. I know mine. Only you know yours.

When we read that scripture on Christ's Passion, being present in prayer to the most horrific death that anyone has ever experienced, we can know two things. First, we know that Jesus Christ, both fully man and fully divine, felt abandoned in his moment of greatest need, most acute loneliness, and deepest suffering. He knew what it meant to ask of a good and loving God, *Where are you? How could you let this happen to me?*

And the second thing we can know is this: God was there. God the Father was there with God the Son as he hung on the Cross for hours. In your darkest moments of suffering, God was there with you, too.

This can be hard to understand, or nearly impossible to believe in light of the depths of the suffering you have faced. Your head may know that God was present, but your heart may not believe it. And so, this week I invite you to ask God to reveal himself to you in that moment. To go back to that time and ask Christ to show you his face in it. To walk with God through that moment or season and invite him to give you a revelation of his love for you then, his nearness in your suffering, his awareness of your every emotion.

Perhaps you will walk through a few different touchpoints in your life this week. Perhaps there is more than one moment that you need to go back to, to sit with Christ in that moment of darkness and allow a revelation of his presence and love for you in that moment to change it. To reshape it. To heal it. To restore it. To reset your broken bones, your broken heart, your broken spirit; to speak to you clearly, "I have not abandoned you. I have not forsaken you."

Step into healing with Christ in the coming days. Where there is darkness, he brings light. Where his presence is, there is safety.

Where his love is, there is stillness. Let the refuge of his presence be a place of peace for you as you walk the road of healing with him in trust and in peace.

"And behold, I am with you always, until the end of the age" (Mt 28:20).

SOUL EXERCISES

1. Take the time to revisit those places and feelings of being abandoned by God. Allow yourself to walk there in prayer with Christ, and let him reveal himself to you in a new way in the midst of that suffering and pain.
2. Sit with the scene of the Passion (Lk 23:26–49) this week, and pray most especially with that moment when Jesus called out to the Father in agony. What does this scene bring up in your heart? What is the Lord speaking to you through it?

YOUR HEART'S PRAYER THIS WEEK

Jesus, I know you never abandon me, but there are times when it has truly felt as if you have. I invite you and give you permission to take me back to those moments of my life when I felt like you were not there with me. Reveal to me your presence in those moments, in that season. Show me your face in the midst of my past and current sufferings. Awaken my heart to see that you knew the pain of feeling forgotten and abandoned, that you understand and

have compassion for my feelings of desertion and sorrow. Amen.

Week 11

Make It Meaningful

Along with motherhood comes monotony. The tasks I am required to complete each day can become very tedious. Whether it's doing another load of laundry, changing another diaper, unloading the dishwasher again, or washing pots and pans after dinner every night, it can feel as if the list of chores is never-ending and never-changing. And unless you're a fancy jet-setter flying all over the world for a big meeting every week, I imagine you feel the same way at times. Whether that's heading to the same job, walking the same halls, getting on the same bus, going to the same locker, or sitting in the same classroom, you may find the routine burdensome.

One night, exasperated over another evening of scrubbing pots after putting Zion to bed, I felt a rush of the wisdom of the Holy Spirit as this question flashed across my heart: *What if I changed these monotonous chores into opportunities for prayer?*

Years ago, I was sitting with my friend Sr. Francesca of the Lamb of God, who lives in a convent in New York. She said that her duties in the convent had recently changed and that she was now responsible for more cleaning, including scrubbing all the toilets in the building. As she shared this with me, without missing a beat she said with her infectious joy, "If scrubbing toilets is what I am called to do to bring glory to God, then I praise him in it!"

I couldn't help but realize just how different my own perspective was. Where I was frustrated by just about every mundane task in my life, Sr. Francesca viewed cleaning toilets as a way to glorify God. St. Teresa of Avila touched on this idea as she spoke to the nuns in her convent about finding the Lord even in the kitchen: "Oh then, my daughters, let there be no neglect: but when obedience calls you to exterior employments (as, for example, into the kitchen, *amidst the pots and dishes*), remember that *our Lord goes along with you*, to help you both in your interior and exterior duties."

We can find the Lord even among the pots and dishes, she said. So, I took St. Teresa's words literally and began the practice of choosing a person to pray for with every pot I scrubbed in

the evening. Each pan was an opportunity to pray for a different person, whoever I knew needed prayer at that time. As the soap foamed and I scrubbed, I said, "Lord, bring (friend's name) peace. Lead her away from the point of despair. Draw her close to you and comfort her heart in her suffering." In this way, I found the Lord among the pots and pans. I invited him into my chores and let my chores become prayers. Not only did this practice help me convert my selfish complaints to loving intercession for others, but it also gave me a joyful spirit as I did my daily duty.

In all of life's tasks, we can ask ourselves, who can I pray for as I do this? As I walk to my locker, as I change this diaper, as I begin this sports practice, as I cook this dinner, as I fold this load of clothes, as I drive this commute, who will I pray for? Routine becomes meaningful when we make it meaningful. Chores become prayers when we make them so. All of a sudden, we *do* have time to pray even in the midst of hectic to-do lists and terribly busy schedules because we make those tasks moments of connection with the Lord.

So do not despair at the tedium of your life. Look at all the little tasks you will do throughout this week, and transform them into something meaningful. Use every task as an opportunity to give glory to Jesus, just like Sr. Francesca, and watch your entire day change.

SOUL EXERCISES

1. What are some of the routine boxes you have to check off every day? Do they include changing diapers, cooking dinner, going to class, clocking in at work? Who can you pray for as you do these tasks this week?
2. This week, identify at least two areas in your life where you can make your work a prayer. Write them down and try it for a week. Make the effort to pray throughout those tasks this week. Notice how your prayer changes them, and changes you.

YOUR HEART'S PRAYER THIS WEEK

Jesus, there are many moments of monotony in my life. I don't want to wish my days away, dreaming of a more exciting or fanciful life, mindlessly checking boxes on my to-do list. Awaken my heart to these moments of my everyday schedule, these moments of fulfilling my vocation, these moments that seem to mean nothing. Help me turn them into sacred moments to connect with you throughout my day. Amen.

Week 12

Silence the
Self-Loathing

Imagine an artist working for forty weeks, day and night, on a project he has thought about for a very long time. Imagine him pouring his creativity, heart, and soul into this project. Imagine that at some point, even many years down the road after the work has been completed, someone says to the artist, "Wow, what an ugly work you made there. It's hideous! What were you thinking?"

I imagine the artist would be more than slightly hurt or offended after all the effort and passion he poured into that piece.

Is it not the same when you speak ugly words to yourself in the presence of our God, who carefully crafted you for many months in his image and likeness?

Your Creator hears every utterance of your mouth and heart. To belittle yourself is to knock his creativity, his vision, and his unique design for you.

When I was in high school, my confidence was up one day and down the next. It ebbed and flowed as my acne came and went, as my body changed, as I grew into the woman I am today. During a particularly low season, when I was struggling badly with my self-esteem, I made up a little song that I sang to myself as I drove to school. "I-I-I-I am the ugliest person ali-i-ive," I would belt out in my 1985 Chevy Blazer. I would sing it over and over again in a strange melody, typically on days when I was dealing with bad acne or something of the like. I look back and want to weep that I sang this lie out loud into the air so often.

A few months ago, while I was spending time with my younger sister, I started speaking negatively about myself, something along the lines of my being an inconvenience to other people, and she immediately said firmly but lovingly, "Stop talking." She didn't say, "That's not true!" or "Don't be silly!" She said, "Stop talking," and I knew what she meant by that. She didn't want to hear me say negative things about myself when even I knew those things weren't true. Now it is something my sister and I have adopted into our conversations. When one of us is speaking negatively in this way,

the other says with directness and immediacy, "Stop talking." We both know that sometimes we speak the ugliest words to ourselves.

When we belittle ourselves, it not only hurts us; it hurts the Lord. And if we don't recognize that this kind of self-talk harms us, we allow it to increase in volume and frequency. If left unchecked, it can become so loud in our heads that we don't hear the voice of God, whose words about what he created are always good and beautiful.

Sadly, as I sang my high-school morning commute song, I was drowning out the song that heaven was and is still singing over me—the song that never stops speaking of the beauty that is a child of God, crafted with care by his glorious hands. It is difficult work to choose to lean into the voice of God, the voice of love, the voice that says you are made good and beautiful, but it is work that must be done. And it is important to let the voice of God influence the way we speak to ourselves.

It can take much longer than a week to rearrange the lies you have believed and spoken to yourself for years. So, this week I invite you to a first step into consciousness of the way you speak to yourself. The first step in the rewiring of lies is to realize that the Lord never created you to talk to yourself that way.

This week is a time to be aware and put a halt to negative self-talk when it begins—to tell yourself, even out loud, "Stop talking," and pray for the Lord to give you the grace to speak positive words to yourself.

This week you may come to realize that these lies are sown deeply into your heart from your childhood or from your past. Maybe you have believed for twenty years that you are a failure because a teacher, parent, or other relative told you this when you were small, and you adopted this lie as part of your deep-seated beliefs about who you are. May this be the week you take the time to sit with the Lord and realize that the way you speak to yourself is deeply affecting your life. If you need to talk to a trusted friend or

a counselor about this, may you gather the courage to do just that, to begin to tear down the negativity and rebuild your self-image. Christ wants you to do this work. He wants you to make this effort because of the truth of who you are, a beloved child of God.

As you sit with the Lord this week, memorize and tuck these scriptures into your heart to combat any temptation to speak ugly words to yourself:

"Yet, Lord, you are our father; we are the clay and you our potter: we are all the work of your hand" (Is 64:7).

"Do you not know that you are the temple of God, and that the Spirit of God dwells in you?" (1 Cor 3:16).

"You formed my inmost being; you knit me in my mother's womb. I praise you, because I am wonderfully made; wonderful are your works! My very self you know" (Ps 139:13–14).

SOUL EXERCISES

1. Do you typically speak positively or negatively to yourself? If you speak negatively to yourself, what are some of the things you say? Write them down. Would you say those things to another woman?
2. Take time this week to write a letter from God to you, telling you what he sees in you, and who he made you to be. Ask him to take the pen and speak the truth of who you are in your writing.

YOUR HEART'S PRAYER THIS WEEK

Jesus, I know you did not create me to spend a life-time putting myself down. Give me the grace to be a woman who is confident, humble, graceful, and strong. I want to speak words of life to others, and I want to speak words of life to myself. Each time I am tempted to insult who you made me to be, help me to choose positivity and kindness instead. You make only good and beautiful things. Thank you for creating me as one of them. Amen.

Week 13

Speak Love

I tell you, on the day of judgment
people will render an account for
every careless word they speak.
By your words you will be acquit-
ted, and by your words you will be
condemned.
—Matthew 12:36–37

Last week, I invited you to reflect on the words you speak to yourself that need to be realigned with the way God wants you to speak to yourself. This week, we will look outward at the ways we speak to and about others. Imagine, for a moment, that Jesus comes to you in human form this week, the same man who walked the earth two thousand years ago. Imagine that Jesus invites you to step into a room with him. Imagine that in this room, every positive and negative word you have spoken about other people throughout your life is written on the walls. Imagine that the positive comments are in green and the negative statements are in red.

Imagine standing there with Jesus as you look together at all of these sentences, words, and phrases. What color would the walls be? Mostly green, with a little red, or covered in red with only the slightest bit of green peeking through?

Would you be able to look Jesus in the eyes as you stand next to him in this room? With these words about his beloved friends exposed and brought to light?

Recently, I was walking with Zion on a bike path, and two men rode by on their bicycles. One of them, laughing loudly, said to the other, "I mean, it's just so fun to rip the guy apart, *especially* when he's not there!" I felt like someone had punched me in the stomach. Something about the way these ugly words were said made me deeply upset for the man being talked about—because I have been like that man, ridiculed behind closed doors when I was not present. Have you been like that man, too?

I wondered if the man knew that others made fun of him behind his back. I wondered how he copes with being treated this way. I began to pray for this man immediately, the man they spoke of, and then began to pray for the man who made the ugly remark. Only the hardest of hearts actually *delights* in tearing other people down. But the reality is, I have been the man on the bicycle, too, tearing other people apart with my words when they are not present. Have you been like that man, too?

One of the lies that the devil speaks well and often to women is that gossip is harmless. *It's just fun banter and everyone does it,* the devil slyly convinces us. He encourages us to believe, *It's no big deal.* Oh, but it is. It really is.

Gossip hurts the heart of Jesus—and even though I don't always love him perfectly, I love Jesus. And I want to honor him—in my heart, in my actions, and in my words. When my words about another don't honor that person, they do not honor God. Women who know who they are, and whose they are, speak words of life and love about others.

We only have to look as far as this week's verse, Matthew 12:36–37, to see that we will have to make an account before the Lord for every word we utter. I wonder, sometimes, what that moment will be like for me. It is really scary.

So, this week is about good words and green walls. I want to stand with Jesus in a room covered with the color green and be unafraid to lock eyes with him rather than be ashamed to even glance over at him. I want to be able to look him in the eyes to say,

In the one life on earth I was given by you, I spoke love.

I spoke peace.

I spoke beauty.

I spoke the truth of Jesus Christ with my words about others.

I made a point in every moment to raise up instead of tear down the kingdom of God on earth.

I want to be that woman—and I imagine and hope that you do, too—who is striving to be like Christ in all things, and in all things to take that green paintbrush and speak beautiful words to and about others. May this week and the rest of our lives be an effort to stand with Jesus face-to-face and be pleased with the words we speak and the way in which we speak these words about each one of his beloved sons and daughters.

SOUL EXERCISES

1. How do you speak about others? Take some time in prayer to close your eyes and imagine yourself in that room with God. Look back not only on the color of the words you spoke, but also on the specific things you said.
2. Recall a time when you heard that someone was speaking negatively about you. How did it make you feel? Reflect on how the words you speak about others would make them feel if they heard you saying them.
3. Has anything come up in your prayer and contemplation this week that you need to apologize for? Consider taking that step of humility and making that apology.

YOUR HEART'S PRAYER THIS WEEK

Jesus, I want to spend my life speaking words of life and love to and about others. I want to be able to stand with you in that room looking at green walls, and I know I need to make some changes for that to happen. Help me to overcome my insecurities and tendency to compare. Awaken my heart to see each person as my brother or sister in Christ so that I may lift them up in every word I speak. Amen.

**Week
14**

Have Mercy
on Yourself

My husband and I moved recently, and in preparation for the move I went through all my belongings in order to throw away the things I did not want to bring to our new home. While shuffling through papers, I found a letter that I had written to myself.

I wrote this letter of forgiveness to myself in 2013. It was about one and a half pages long, and I remember how free I felt the moment I signed my name at the bottom.

In the Christian life, we often talk about the importance of extending mercy and forgiveness to others. Forgiving others is an integral part of a life with the Lord, as we say every time we pray the Our Father, "Forgive us our debts, as we forgive our debtors" (Mt 6:12). I planned on writing a week's reflection on forgiving others, but when I began to pray about it, I realized it is more likely that we need a week devoted to forgiving ourselves.

It is no secret that we are often harder on ourselves than we are on other people. In relationships, at times we have made mistakes, caused pain or division, betrayed others, or sinned in a way that has lifelong consequences. Sometimes we hold on to the anger we feel toward ourselves for these choices for weeks, months, or even years.

Women hold so many things against themselves. In the black of night, many women struggle to stop thinking about the regrets that keep them from sleeping. So many women don't believe they deserve joy in their lives because of what they have done. The things we hold on to range from little to big, extremely serious to less serious—but they are all important. Here are the situations I hear women struggling with most often:

- ♥ Betraying a friend and ruining the friendship
- ♥ Being unfaithful to a good man by cheating
- ♥ Making a poor decision in the raising of a child
- ♥ Giving a cold shoulder to a relative in need
- ♥ Having sex with a boyfriend after vowing to save sex for marriage

- ♥ Exchanging bitter, hurtful, and resentful words with a loved one
- ♥ Quitting something rather than persevering in it
- ♥ Causing harm in the family or deep pain to one or both parents by a choice made

Maybe it was just one sentence you said, off the cuff, and that one sentence has turned into years of regret. How easy it can be to forgive others, to allow them to forgive us—but how easy it is, too, to berate ourselves for the mistakes we have made, to even go so far as to hate ourselves for the messes we have created or the pain we have caused.

And here's the thing . . . the enemy wants you to live like this. The enemy wants you to carry around self-hatred. The enemy wants you to ceaselessly lament over your poor choices. But our loving God does not.

It is not the will of God for you to live like this. It is not the will of God that you live with bitterness in your heart toward yourself or even go so far as to hate yourself.

The will of God for your life is freedom and peace within your heart. God desires greatly that you accept your humanity and learn to forgive yourself in order to live in joy.

In 2013, I was holding on to regret from a dating relationship I had allowed to continue for far too long, and I was very angry at myself. For months I lived in disbelief at my own blindness and my lack of courage to end the relationship, often crying myself to sleep over my stupidity. I felt chained down by the resentment I carried toward myself. I finally came to a point where I saw clearly that this was not what God had created me for or how he desired me to live.

So, I wrote that letter of forgiveness to myself. I prayed before I wrote it, that in my writing Christ would truly set me free and that I would sincerely be able to forgive and let go. And as I wrote, the Lord brought me clear vision to accept the fact that I am a sinner, that I have made mistakes and am bound to make more in life.

He also showed me that life is a constant process of learning, that repentance and mercy are real and available to me, and that I can always decide to begin again. I wrote out in plain language what I wanted to forgive myself for, the specific choices, the pain I had caused others and myself, holding nothing back. When I found that letter recently, I felt the same rush of freedom I experienced when I signed off *"Love, Emily"* on that piece of paper.

This week is an invitation to explore those places in your heart where you are unable to have mercy on yourself. I invite you to write your own letter—to step into freedom by putting it all down on paper. It's not easy . . . we'd rather bury those resentments we hold against ourselves, forget about them, pretend they are not there.

But they are there. And they are worth looking at, reflecting upon, and working through with your Savior.

Whatever has come up in your heart, I know you have carried it for far too long, and God desires freedom for you. Take the time this week to pray, to write, to forgive yourself and step into peace.

SOUL EXERCISE

For what in your life do you need to forgive yourself? It could be one thing, or a few. Take some time
to pray about what those things are. Then write a
letter of self-forgiveness in the presence of God.
Include everything; hold nothing back. Ask the Lord
to be with you as you write, to help you step into
the peace your heart longs for and that he desires
for you.

YOUR HEART'S PRAYER
THIS WEEK

Jesus, show me how I have been unable to forgive
myself. Show me how I resent myself for things I
did or wish I had done. You have asked me to forgive seventy-times-seven times—please give me the
courage to extend that forgiveness to myself and
live in the freedom you have created me for. Amen.

Week 15

Go Bravely

I can do all things in him
who strengthens me.
—Philippians 4:13 (RSV)

I am trying to cultivate a generation of young women who believe in themselves and in who God created them to be. It is beautiful. It is fulfilling. It is a great struggle on many days, and I often fall prey to the lie that "I can't." Perhaps there is something in your life that you are struggling to believe that you can do—perhaps the words "I can't" are leading the charge in your everyday life or in a specific situation.

One of the most wonderful surprises in life is stumbling upon a scene soaked in beauty, dripping with the heart and grace of God when you least expect it. Years ago, I joined Daniël at the beach near our house to watch him surf. What I thought would be a normal afternoon became a few hours that will remain with me forever. When we walked down to the shore, we came upon a group of people in wheelchairs sitting on the sand. It didn't take long to see that these people weren't there just to watch and enjoy the ocean. They were there to surf, too. A special team was there to facilitate the surfing. First, the team outfitted each of the men and women with wet suits. Then, the team members loaded some of the individuals onto their backs and carried them to the water. One man crawled on his hands and knees out to the waves while a young man carried his board behind him.

I saw one team member lift a young man with a blond topknot who looked about my age onto his back, while another brought out his red board. They placed him in the water with his board and handed him his double-sided oar. The man began to paddle out, headed valiantly toward the waves. The swell rushed in quickly and crashed into him, immediately flipping him over. My heart raced until I saw his head pop out of the water, and I watched as he pulled himself back onto his board, pulling his legs back into place one at a time with his arms. He began to paddle out again and was flipped over by another wave.

He struggled to get past the break in the waves as they kept coming. It happened a third time. He flipped his board over and

pulled himself back on with all his might, again and again. And then I witnessed him make it past the break and out to the surf. He turned around and caught his first wave. I wish you could have been there to see it.

I watched each of these individuals out in the water, battling and gritting their teeth and fighting past the break against all odds. For an hour I watched this scene soaked with beauty. I wiped tears that fell behind my sunglasses as I witnessed these men and women take the brushes of their lives and paint a picture of what resilience and determination look like for us all.

God knew I needed to witness this event because the lie of "I can't" played a big role in my life at the time. How often we believe those two ugly words that the enemy uses to get us to give in and give up . . . *I can't lead, I can't finish this project, I can't make a different choice, I can't stop giving in to sin . . .*

In his letter to the Philippians, St. Paul teaches us what should be at the forefront of our hearts in every situation: "I have the strength for everything through him who empowers me" (4:13). I sobbed many evenings in my bed in college, thinking, *I can't keep living my faith here.* I cried in the dark of many nights as Zion woke up fussing, thinking, *I can't get up to feed him once more.* I have shaken in fear at the role of leadership God has given me, saying to myself, *I can't possibly be the leader these women need.* But in that moment at the beach, my heart was imprinted with an image I will not forget—the image of a young man with a blond topknot on a red board who does not give up, who does not let anything get in the way of his mission and his passion. He goes back out again and again because he remembers that feeling of flying down the waves. He is an example for us all—a man who was likely told, "You can't," "That will be impossible," "It's not worth trying," but who pushes through and says with his life as he flies jubilantly down a wave, "Yes, I can."

I will never forget that day when the wheelchairs next to me sat empty and God taught me how to battle against the lie that "I can't." I invite you into reflection this week: Where are you believing this lie? Where in your life have you given up? Where in your life has God called you to something and you have believed that you can't do it because you are trying to do it on your own strength? Where is God asking you to rearrange your belief that you can't into the conviction that you can?

The young man on the red board didn't speak any words, and I will likely never meet him, but he convicted my heart by his life that it is indeed through Christ, with Christ, and in Christ that I can do all things.

SOUL EXERCISES

1. Where have you fallen prey to the lie that you "can't"? Where have you given in to the idea that you're not capable, or just not good enough?
2. If you run into a situation this week that you think you cannot handle, speak out loud or in your heart the words of Philippians 4:13—"I can do all things through Christ who strengthens me." See how saying this verse changes your beliefs or attitude in this moment. Adopting this practice into your life can change your approach to everything.

YOUR HEART'S PRAYER
THIS WEEK

Jesus, there are so many days when I struggle to believe that I can do all things through you. I feel defeated as I depend on myself rather than you. I get discouraged by my lack of progress and feel like bowing to the lie that "I can't." Give me the grace to live Philippians 4:13 with my whole heart—to speak it out loud in moments of defeat or discouragement and in times of desperation and struggle. Give me the courage to proclaim the truth out loud, the

truth that will remain forever, that I can do all things through you who strengthens me. Amen.

Week
16

Love the Poor

The streets of Los Angeles today are lined with tents, thousands of tents the homeless have pitched in order to have some shelter, a place to call home. They are people, just like you and me—people who have perhaps fallen to addiction, fallen on hard times, fallen into a season or a lifetime of living without a roof over their heads. Many see these people as a disturbance, an annoyance, an inconvenience, cluttering the city with their homelessness.

When was the last time you asked a homeless person their name? Pope Francis speaks frequently on the humanity of the poor and how important it is to treat them with dignity. He stated in a recent interview that it was imperative for Christians to "see another person not as a pathology or social condition, but as a human, with a life whose value is equal to your own." I thought hard about it—when was the last time I saw the personhood of a homeless person on the side of the road begging for money? When was the last time they were treated like a person with a story and a soul?

So the next time I saw a homeless man, I remembered. He was standing at the exit of a freeway in Los Angeles with a beat-up guitar slung over his back. He was a shaggy man who looked about my age. I reached out my car window and gave him a few dollars and said, "Hi! I'm Emily. What's your name?"

"I'm Ryan," he said as he reached out to take the money from my hand. And in an instant, I realized that someone chose that name for him. His mother had named him Ryan, just like mine had named me Emily. And in that moment, I did not see a ragged man with matted hair; I saw a person with a story, and a mom and dad who had given him life.

And is that not the reality of you and me—and our homeless brothers and sisters—that we are all children of God? That we are, each one of us, human beings in need of love and compassion, made in the image and likeness of the almighty God? To love the poor is to love Jesus himself, but often I overlook them or don't step out to love them intentionally and purposefully. But as followers

of Jesus, we can be a small part of the solution every day. He very specifically asks us in scripture to care for the poor: "If someone who has worldly means sees a brother in need and refuses him compassion, how can the love of God remain in him?" (1 Jn 3:17).

"Then the king will say to those on his right, 'Come, you who are blessed by my Father. Inherit the kingdom prepared for you from the foundation of the world. For I was hungry and you gave me food, I was thirsty and you gave me drink, a stranger and you welcomed me, naked and you clothed me, ill and you cared for me, in prison and you visited me'" (Mt 25:34–36).

The poor in our midst are mothers and daughters and sons and fathers, people with feelings and dreams and desires and emotions. There are so many ways we can reach out to them and love them. First, we can treat the homeless as people like you and me—people with names and hearts and stories. Second, we can fill a need for them, in whatever way we can. Perhaps that means packing a few snack bags in our car or backpack to hand out when we cross paths with someone in need. Perhaps that means giving the last twenty dollars we have in our wallet to be Christ's provision in one short exchange. Perhaps that means volunteering at a homeless shelter one day this week, or donating good clothes to a local shelter in need. Perhaps it just means having a conversation with someone.

Let us love the poor this week in a profound outpouring of the love of Jesus Christ. May your love be so radical that those you encounter know in a new way that God is real and that in the midst of their struggle, *he cares.*

SOUL EXERCISES

1. What is one concrete way you can love the poor this week? Go out of your way, take the time, and make the effort to do it.
2. Have you ever had an impactful experience with the poor? Whether it was with someone in a foreign country or someone down the street, contemplate why that experience made an impression on you and what God revealed to your heart.

YOUR HEART'S PRAYER
THIS WEEK

Jesus, you have a deep love for the poor. Help me to have that same love. Shape me into a woman who gives food to the hungry, clothes to the naked, and drink to the thirsty. Awaken my heart to see the humanity of the poor and to share in that humanity whenever I can. As I extend my hand to the poor, help them to see not my hand, but yours. Amen.

Week 17

Shift Your Perspective

I sat next to a man on a plane in first class once who complained about everything. Absolutely everything. I have had hard days myself when I've chosen to voice my frustrations, but by this man's tenth complaint to the flight attendant and to those of us around him, I thought my eyes would bulge out of my head. Have you ever encountered someone like this and wanted to say, "Can't you just be grateful?"

Complaints come easy in a culture that pushes us toward constant self-centeredness and obsession with things going our way. Some days I find so many things to complain about—it's hot, the dryer is taking too long, my flight is delayed, and I'm uncomfortable and crammed in the back of the plane. Are *you* the person who complains often, who people want to turn to and say, "Can't you just be grateful?"

I have a picture on my phone of a man in the army holding his baby daughter at the airport before he leaves on deployment. He is weeping as he tells her goodbye, knowing that she will grow and change in many ways before he returns home. I follow a beautiful woman online whose son was born three days after mine. When her child was just a few months old, he was diagnosed with leukemia. They have been in the hospital for nearly an entire year. When I wake up in the morning after being up with Zion many times during the night, I know I have nothing to complain about—that either of these people would have given much to hold their baby all night long. To have the eyes to see the lives of others—this is what keeps me from complaining. Perspective.

When we step into perspective, we step into awakening. It is essential, if we want to live lives of gratitude to God rather than complaint, to keep perspective. Not in a way that says, "Wow, I'm *so* glad I am not that person!" but in a way that reminds us how trivial and unimportant are many of the things we complain about.

The saints in the Catholic Church can teach us about perspective. Many saints endured enormous suffering and carried

impossibly heavy crosses, but they showed us how to live awake to what God was doing and asking of them even in the midst of deep suffering. One saint who didn't complain about his conditions and struggles was St. Maximilian Kolbe, who led fellow prisoners in songs of worship to God as he starved to death in the Auschwitz concentration camp. Another was St. Joan of Arc, who herself removed an arrow that struck her in the neck in order to carry on her mission of leading thousands of men in battle. She kept her spirits high and continually cheered her soldiers on. Another example is fourteen-year-old St. José Sánchez del Río, who was forced to walk the streets of Mexico with his feet skinned as a prisoner for his faith. He never stopped giving praise and thanks to God. Each of these saints had perspective—the perspective of eyes and heart fixed heavenward.

This week is all about cultivating perspective. To resist the temptation to complain about my own struggles is to fight back against a culture of selfishness instead of getting sucked into it. To step into self-awareness, I can ask myself, "Why am I sharing this?" each time I want to complain to someone. If the honest answer is "Just to complain," I can stop myself from saying a word.

When my heart is filled with compassion, there is no room for complaining. When I lean into perspective, there is no room for pouting. To change my perspective is to change my vision and outlook on life—and that changes everything.

SOUL EXERCISE

Fast from complaining. Pay close attention this week
to those areas and situations where you have a tendency to complain. When a complaint wells up within you, stop yourself before speaking and reevaluate
your perspective.

YOUR HEART'S PRAYER THIS WEEK

Jesus, please grant me perspective in all things.
Sometimes I complain about the most trivial things.
Help me to leave behind my complaints and live
with deep faith and wisdom. Awaken my heart to
the beauty and goodness in my life, and show me
how my life's obstacles and crosses can be offered
up to you, for my good and for your glory. Amen.

Week 18

Find Your
Worth in God

It was a Tuesday morning. I had worked hard writing a post on social media that I thought would be particularly impactful for women. I pressed post and checked back again soon to see how it was doing. I checked back again, and again, refreshing the page every few minutes. And in an instant, it hit me like a bag of bricks.

I thought, *How desperate I am for love, for attention, for validation from other people that what I have to say is important.* And I act out of this desperation. Sometimes you probably do too.

We are desperate for many things—love, attention from guys, achievements, the regard of other people, fame, acclaim, worldly comforts, gratitude from people we went out of our way to help. All it takes is one scroll through YouTube to find thousands of videos about how to get noticed (whether by a guy or by people in general), to grow your following, to get rich, to achieve worldly success and accolades. One look at a magazine stand shows us all the ways we can achieve the worldly things that are supposed to bring us satisfaction. Our world squeezes every dollar it can out of our desperate struggles for attention and validation of who we are. What the Lord has awakened me to see is that this desperation I feel is, at its core, a search for my worth. It is a search for someone to tell me I am valuable and loved.

As I refreshed the engagement count on that post over and over, in that moment of realization of how often I grasp at finite things to find my worth, I heard the Lord's voice ring clear as a bell in my heart as he told me, "I did not create you for a life of desperation. I created you to find your worth in me."

The Creator of the universe did not create *you* for a life of desperation, but a life of security, a life rooted in the knowledge that you are valuable because you are created and loved by him: "And you shall be secure, because there is hope; you shall look round you and lie down in safety" (Jb 11:18).

I fell to my knees as I came to see that I was operating out of desperation in so many areas in my life, floundering around in

search of something from which I could derive my worth. I knew I had hit my breaking point. I realized that in this rearranging the Lord was doing in my heart, I first needed to pinpoint the places where I was grasping at things like someone drowning. I needed to take an inventory, to reflect with self-awareness on my motives for doing things. I knew that I needed to hand it all over to him and begin to reorder what I was doing in my life. But I did not know where to start. So I started with a simple prayer . . . *Lord, lead me from a life of desperation into a life of security in you. Help me to believe and know that my worth and value as a woman lie in you.*

When I pray this prayer, the Lord invites me to fix my desperate, searching eyes and heart on his great act of sacrifice and love . . . he invites me to look at the Cross. The answer to my search for worth will always be found in the Cross. This is the answer to every struggle of desperation I will ever experience.

When you are desperate for someone to love you, desperate for someone to tell you that you are worthy of love, look to the Cross and see Jesus say, "I love you," with his life.

When you are desperate to be thought of by someone, *anyone*, look to the Cross and see that the Lord thought of you there and has been thinking of you since the beginning of time.

When you are desperate for someone to see you, to know you, to tell you that you're worthy, look to the Cross. It is proof that we have security in his heart and in his love for each one of us.

And so, this week I ask you, in what area of your life are you acting out of desperation? Where do you long for people to think or say, *Wow, she's really smart, she's really doing big things, what an impressive photo, she's beautiful, she's so successful, she is important, she is worthy* . . . Where are you looking for your worth? The Lord doesn't want you to live in desperation. He wants you to live in the security he provides because you can truly *thrive* in that security and find the joy, comfort, and satisfaction only he can bring. True

joy makes itself manifest in our lives when we operate out of security in who we are and who we were created to be in him.

It is up to each of us to step back and do this hard work, to take this inventory, and to begin to make changes. The world does not want us to work on this. The world wants us to watch videos, to consume media, to buy everything it says will help us achieve satisfaction, to attempt to find our value in every fleeting thing so we consume even more of it. But the Lord wants you to step back and enter into the rearranging and reworking of your heart this week.

It's a week that requires a hard look at some things we may not want to look at, but this digging will lead to new growth and, ultimately, to a new ability to thrive in the love Christ has for each of us. When we pinpoint the areas of desperation in our lives, we can begin to root them out, starting with that simple prayer . . . *Lord, lead me from a life of desperation into a life of security in you.*

SOUL EXERCISES

1. Picture yourself at the foot of the Cross of Christ. Now recall the sources you turn to for validation. Imagine laying each of them down at the foot of the Cross and pray, "I surrender everything to you, Jesus."
2. Take deep breaths and release your insecurities and feelings of desperation. Lay it all down at the foot of the Cross.
3. Keep your gaze fixed on the Lord and his love for you. Pray, "May this be the one and only place I search for my worth and security for the rest of my life."

YOUR HEART'S PRAYER
THIS WEEK

Loving Jesus, show me the places in my life where I am acting out of desperation. Instead of speaking and acting from a place of insecurity, help me to calm my heart and trust in you. Be with me in my every choice, and give me confidence in your love. Help me find my worth in you and you alone. Amen.

Week 19

Listen with Love

Know this, my dear brothers:
everyone should be quick to hear,
slow to speak, slow to wrath.
—James 1:19

Listening—attentive, mindful listening—is a lost art in our culture. Not only have we lost the ability to listen completely, but we've also forgotten how to love by simply being totally present to another human being.

Most of the time we half listen. Much of our listening involves looking at people and hearing bits and pieces of what they are saying while thinking about how we will to respond to them. We assume that we've taken in all the info and therefore don't really need to pay attention anymore. Our minds move on to other thoughts and ideas. At least that's how it happens for me. I was in complete denial at first, but when I actually took stock of how well I practice attentiveness while listening—by keeping my mind focused on the person in front of me and not allowing it to wander off—I realized that I only half listen.

It is a prideful habit because when I assume I get the point of what someone else is saying to me, I'm basically concluding that my thoughts and ideas are superior to whatever my brother or sister in Christ has to say.

What does half listening look like for you? Maybe you find yourself scrolling on your phone while someone talks to you. Or do you browse on your computer while having a phone conversation? Do you insert an "mhmm, mhmm" here and there, to make the speaker think you are really paying attention to what they have to say? Half listening (really, *not listening*) can take on many different forms, but we're all guilty of it in some fashion.

Once, when I was on a retreat in high school, one of my school counselors shared her experience of practicing how to listen attentively. She said that any time she speaks with a person, she wants that person to feel as though she had an index card with the message You Are Important taped to her forehead. She hoped that by giving her full and undivided attention to that person, they would know they are seen, heard, and loved.

Is that not what Christ does for us, and models for us? "When you call me, and come and pray to me, I will listen to you" (Jer 29:12).

I learn about the way I should listen from the way the Lord listens to me. He never interjects his thoughts before I finish sharing. He never stops me while I'm talking. He never listens to phrases or words here and there, excited to get his point or advice in as soon as I'm done. He listens to everything that I have to say—every single word.

He listens fully. Completely. And while he is listening, his face is not turned away with one ear leaned in while doing something else. The Lord's gaze is turned completely, fully, on me. He knows that his precious children deserve his full attention.

Listening to people and looking them in the eyes is a tangible way to live out the love of Christ. It is also uncommon and refreshing. We notice when people really, truly care in our world today—because sadly, many people are too busy with their own affairs to make time for others.

Love people in your listening this week and beyond. Show them the face of Jesus Christ as you look at them while they speak, as if to say with your whole heart, "You are important to me, and I am listening."

SOUL EXERCISES

1. This week, intentionally and deliberately, give full attention to every person you are with. Is this something you do always, or is it challenging for you?

2. Have you heard of the practice of friends getting together and stacking their phones in the center of the table so they pay full attention to one another? This week, I challenge you to adopt this practice into your life. If you are with someone else, put away your phone. Be fully present to that person.

YOUR HEART'S PRAYER THIS WEEK

Jesus, thank you for always listening to me, during every second of my day and in every season of my life. Help me to love others well by giving them my full attention when I am with them. Give me the grace to listen as attentively to others as you do to me, with patience and without pride. Amen.

Week 20

Unclench
Your Fists

It was a very tender moment of prayer I will never forget. During a time of guided reflection on a retreat, in my mind I had a vision of Jesus approaching me lovingly and lifting up both of my hands from my sides as he stood in front of me. My hands were clenched in tight fists. Jesus looked at my fists, and he looked at me, and with his gentle and loving hands began to unfurl my fingers, one by one.

I knew well why my fists were clenched so tightly. I was relying on myself in every facet of my life—my ministry, my motherhood, my vocation to marriage. I was trying to do everything myself, without relying on him for help, for strength, for guidance. I was running close to burnout as I poured myself into all of these avenues of ministry and vocation without ever thinking of the Lord. My fists before the Lord were an embarrassing symbol of control, of a lack of surrender to his leadership and provision, and as he opened my hands with his own, I realized how much of my life I spend with clenched fists. I cling tightly to so much in a pitiful attempt at control.

We were not created to control.

Clenched fists in the presence of God can symbolize many different things. Sometimes fists are tightly closed because they are holding on to something—maybe a dream, maybe a possession, maybe something from the past, maybe the pen that is writing the story of your life that you have snatched from the Lord because you think he is writing too slowly or has got the story wrong. Clenched fists can represent anger, greed, or fear. Whatever the reason for clenched fists, in the presence of a sovereign, all-loving God, they reflect the opposite of trust.

Jesus opened my hands, and in this action he said, *Trust me. Rely on me. Depend on me. Let me write the story. Let me lead you. Let me guide you in all things.*

Are you living your life with clenched fists?

Sometimes it is not even both of our hands that are closed. Sometimes we have one hand open to Jesus in front of us, believing

that we trust fully in the Lord and his plan for our life. But at the same time, we have one fist clenched and hidden behind our back, holding on to control, or fear, or our plans, or something the Lord has asked us to hand over to him, something we have not yet relinquished to his sovereignty. We may even convince ourselves that Jesus does not know what we have hidden behind our backs—when in truth, he knows everything we are keeping from him.

Often we hold on tightly for fear of what will happen if we surrender completely. A few years ago, I learned a simple prayer that Henri Nouwen, the well-known Dutch priest and writer, shared with the world: *Lord, unclench my fists.*

In his writing on our tendency to live with fists tightly clenched, Nouwen said, "Each time you dare to let go and to surrender one of those many fears, your hand opens a little and your palms spread out in a gesture of receiving. You must be patient, of course, very patient until your hands are completely open. It is a long spiritual journey of trust, for behind each fist another one is hiding, and sometimes the process seems endless. Much has happened in your life to make all those fists and at any hour of the day or night you might find yourself clenching your fists again out of fear."

The process of unfurling our hands before the Lord can be long and arduous. It can take months, even years, to identify what we hold on to, what we refuse to surrender, areas in which we trust the Lord half-heartedly or not at all. This week is an invitation into deep prayer with the Lord, prayer to open your hands and surrender everything to him, or prayer for him to show you the clenched fists in your life.

I leave you with a beautiful prayer Henri Nouwen wrote of this surrender, of conquering this trouble we have. Pray it again and again, as many times as you need to, until you mean it even with the most hidden places of your heart.

Dear God,

I am so afraid to open my clenched fists!
Who will I be when I have nothing left to
hold on to? Who will I be when I stand
before you with empty hands?

Please help me to gradually open my hands
and to discover that I am not what I own,
but what you want to give me.
And what you want to give me is love—
unconditional, everlasting love.

Amen.

SOUL EXERCISES

1. What are you holding on to in your life? Take time to reflect on this question this week. We all have things we are clinging to that Christ wants us to surrender to him.
2. Sit with that final prayer from Nouwen for a few minutes each day. Imagine Christ himself is with you as you let go of the things that come up in your prayer.

YOUR HEART'S PRAYER
THIS WEEK

Gentle Jesus, here are my hands, here is my heart. Open them so that I may live in your freedom. I surrender all of my hopes, dreams, fears, joys—all of my life—to you. Have your way with it all. Amen.

Week 21

Live
Abundantly

At the time I'm writing this book, I have heard of more tragedy than my heart can handle. Because of my ministry, I'm in touch with families and individuals all over the world, and the tragedy that has taken place within my sphere lately has been unbearable. Two parents of former students died suddenly in car accidents. An old friend in her thirties passed away from cancer. The lives of teens at parishes where I have spoken have been tragically lost. A faithful father of four was diagnosed with cancer and died weeks later. Confusion is deep in the communities affected by these deaths.

As I sit here, I am struck by how quickly death can come, like a thief in the night. Through these shared stories and pain, I have learned repeatedly that our lives can end in one short instant. The life within me is the most fragile thing I possess, yet I, like so many others, act as though I will live forever on this earth.

I'm trying now more than ever to consider how I would spend my time if I were given one more week to live. This might sound like a morbid exercise, but it's my personal and human attempt to bring something good out of sadness and untimely death.

What would I wish I had done differently if someone told me today that my life would end soon? I would wish I had worried less and lived more deeply in faith rather than fear. I would wish that I had smiled at other people more and engaged more fully with them in conversation. I'd wish I had spent less time on my phone and more time looking up at the world. I'd wish I had stressed less about whether God would provide and just trusted that when he says he will, he will. I'd wish I had hurried less and lived each moment more intentionally. I would lament the fact that I had not stopped to watch so many beautiful sunsets. I'd wish I had dared to go beyond the surface in many of my friendships instead of avoiding depth to keep everyone comfortable. I'd wish I'd spent more time celebrating myself rather than focusing on all the things I think are wrong with me. I'd wish I had done more random acts of kindness—like encouraging all those strangers I sometimes felt

the Holy Spirit prompting me to support. I'd wish I had given more and taken less for granted. I would wish I had been better able to let the little things go. I would wish I had lived with more abandon.

When I look at what I'd wish I had done differently, I know that I can change these things *now*. I can let the reality of death shake me from my complacency in living, allow it to wake me up to the truth that my earthly life could be over tomorrow. I can decide from this moment forward to live more radically and more purposefully. I want to live awakened to the fragility of life, and I want to make positive changes. I want to make sense of death by changing the way I live and the way I love.

And I ask you . . . what would your list look like? How would you live differently if you found out this week was your last? I invite you to ponder these questions in your own life. May the fragility of our lives affect the way we live, the way we love, and the way we give.

"Teach us to count our days aright, that we may gain wisdom of heart" (Ps 90:12).

SOUL EXERCISES

1. Do you assume that you will live until you are old? What (if anything) in your life has given you the eyes to see the fragility of our human lives?
2. If you had one more week to live, what would you do differently?

YOUR HEART'S PRAYER THIS WEEK

Jesus, I don't want to live assuming that I'll live forever. Awaken my heart to the fragility of my life—to see that the time to act is now; the time to surrender everything and follow you is now; the day to really, truly live is today. Teach me to act wisely, to slow down, and to pay attention—to sincerely love others by pouring out the love you have shown to me. Amen.

Week
22

Take the
First Step

A few years ago, every afternoon as I walked into the gym, I could hear it from far away. It was the sound of feet skidding loudly on a treadmill. I knew exactly who it was, and he taught me a lesson every single day without saying a word.

He was a teenage boy who could barely walk. He had brown hair, was a bit stocky, and wore blue jeans; he wobbled around with difficulty, relying heavily on a cane. The first few times I saw him at the gym, I watched him stumble over to the treadmill and get on. And he began. He took one slow step after the next. He would do this for long periods of time . . . one by one, he'd put his feet slowly forward.

I saw him frequently, and I knew by the way he stayed on that treadmill that he was dedicated to this, that this was something he had put his mind to and was going to persevere in. I saw him a few times a week over the course of a year. I watched as he progressed slowly, walking a little farther, a little easier. Then I began to go to the gym at night, and I did not see him anymore.

Months went by, and one day I went to the gym in the afternoon. There he was. My heart leapt at seeing this teacher of mine who had no idea how much he had shown me already. I was surprised to see him walking around without his cane. I was amazed moments later when he got on the treadmill.

He got on that thing . . . and he ran.

And in that moment, in his simple act of running, he showed me that nothing is impossible. His feet skidded loudly because he couldn't pick them up all the way, but he ran. I get tears in my eyes writing about it now, watching him in this glorious triumph that seemed so far off not very long before.

I vividly remember the day I first saw him hobbling in and how he put one foot in front of the other, and I am convicted about all the times I haven't wanted to put my foot forward. I remember the days when I have been given a less-than-ideal situation and I haven't wanted to move forward because it seemed unfair, or too

difficult, or even impossible to get through. I know that sometimes it takes forever for me to decide to stand up and get on that impossible life treadmill. And he, through this journey I have watched him navigate, teaches me to stand up, take that first step, and carry on.

It's about putting one foot in front of the other, he says to me without ever saying a word.

I am joyful and overcome with gratitude for this most beautiful and simple lesson he teaches me over and over again. After the first time I saw him run, I began to see him frequently. He and I were at the gym at the same time on most days; he listened to loud folk-rock music and moved his hands like he was playing a great guitar solo as he ran. He wore his blue jeans every day, and on some days, I had the honor of him running next to me, feet skidding loudly while I basked in his grit and perseverance. And while he ran, with the sound of his feet he told me, *Just keep going forward in life. Especially in the worst and most unfair of circumstances. One step at a time. Just. Keep. Going.*

Is there an area in your life where you are stalled out, standing still when you need to take a step forward? Perhaps it is in the area of your health—maybe you need to take a step in the direction of caring for your body or making positive choices in your eating habits. Perhaps you need to take a step in the direction of healing in a relationship, in the discernment of your vocation, in the process of forgiving someone, or in reigniting your relationship with God.

This week I invite you to get on the proverbial treadmill and take the first step. I am certain that young man would look you in the eyes and tell you, "Take the first step, and keep going. I am living proof that not only is it possible; it is worth it."

"Not only that, but we even boast of our afflictions, knowing that affliction produces endurance, and endurance, proven character, and proven character, hope" (Rom 5:3–4).

SOUL EXERCISES

1. Where in your life are you facing a mountain you have to climb and hesitating to take the first step? What is holding you back?
2. Take the first step in climbing that mountain this week. Perhaps it's making an appointment to see a counselor or setting a goal for a healthier lifestyle. If you need some support from a friend in taking this first step, reach out to someone and share with them about it.

YOUR HEART'S PRAYER THIS WEEK

Jesus, it is so easy to stall out and give up when things get difficult, when I am burdened by sufferings and worries about the future. Remind me to take life one day, one step at a time. When I am overwhelmed with my responsibilities, worries, or anxieties, calm my heart. Remind me to place one foot in front of the other, knowing that you walk beside me in all of my days, all of my troubles, and all of my joys. Thank you for walking by my side. I praise you for your faithfulness in every step. Amen.

Week 23

Call Them by Name

We were eating dinner at the Cheesecake Factory one night, with a lovely server whom I'll call Tanya. As she took our order and brought us our food, I could just see it in her eyes. I could see that she was burdened and broken down, trying to make it through this shift to be able to go home and rest.

As she gave us our bill, in a moment of courage I asked her if there was anything she would like us to pray for. She looked surprised, but relieved, and began to share about her life openly with us. Her teenage daughter was struggling with self-harm and getting treatment—they were struggling together, and she was doing her best to keep it all together and make ends meet waiting tables. She was suffering deeply.

So, Tanya stood there while I prayed, and then she got back to work. I will not soon forget that dinner or that moment.

When my siblings and I were young, we wanted to give names to the workers we saw every day. For instance, we named the garbage man Peter. His name wasn't really Peter, but we wanted to pick a name for him. And then we called every garbage man Peter for the rest of our childhood.

I think we sometimes forget that the workers we encounter on a daily basis are people who have stories, who may be struggling, and are people who need to be treated with compassion, care, and patience.

When I worked in a restaurant, I felt like a servant most of the time. Not because I waited on people, but because of how people treated me. Make my coffee. Bring me my food. Wipe the table, please, because we've been waiting for forty minutes. Rarely did people commiserate with my plight as a hostess on a Friday night at a busy restaurant trying my best to get people seated and not overwhelm our servers to the point where their service would be so poor that they wouldn't make a single tip. It was eye-opening to be treated like a servant rather than a person striving to do her job well. As someone who flies a lot, I see people take out their

frustrations on airline employees *all the time.* People get impatient, sometimes for good reason, but they make the employees punching bags for their annoyances—when in most circumstances the employee did *absolutely nothing* to cause the trouble.

Have you ever called a waitress, flight attendant, barista, or bus driver by the name on their name tag? They sometimes look at you, puzzled, as if to say, *How do you know my name?* This week is about intentionally focusing on people like Tanya and Peter who deserve to be treated like persons rather than robots as they make our coffee, check us out at the grocery store, drive the bus, service our car. This week is an invitation to focus on their humanity, to see them the way Christ sees them.

Now, I'm not inviting you to ask every worker what they need prayers for (although you can if you're feeling bold). But I am asking you to treat every service worker you come in contact with this week like a real person with a heart, soul, and story. Consider asking them their name. Don't glide over the question of "How are you?" but perhaps stop for a while to talk with them and thank them cheerfully. It might be the one time that day when someone treats them well. And yet, it is the way we as followers of Jesus should treat every soul woven into the tapestry of our day.

Call them by name. Look them in the eyes. Show them patience. Maybe tip a little extra, if you can. Be Jesus to them, if just for two minutes. Peter. Tanya. Emily. We are all humans, with different jobs and in different seasons. Let us love one another, as indeed we are called to do.

SOUL EXERCISES

1. Go out of your way to have a conversation with a worker in a store or restaurant this week. Ask them sincerely how they are doing and go from there.
2. If you encounter workers with name tags, call them by name, and as you leave, say a simple prayer for them by name.

YOUR HEART'S PRAYER THIS WEEK

Jesus, I thank you with my whole heart for all of the workers I see on a regular basis whom I do not stop to appreciate. Thank you for their hard work to clean my street, to pick up my trash, to make coffee or lunch for me, to stock my grocery store shelves, to serve my table, and so much more. Help me to show cheerful kindness to each person I meet who is working to make my life better. May they see the light of Christ in me as they go about their work. Amen.

**Week
24**

Feel Your
Heart Beat

The discovery of one's purpose seems to have become a grand pursuit these days, the chasing after of an abstract idea rich with meaning. "Purpose" today must be about changing the world and affecting the lives of many people and doing something powerful. Search the keywords "purpose" and "book" together on Amazon, and you'll find thirty thousand book options to help you make this discovery in your own life.

Our world has a seemingly deep desire to nail down what this purpose is for each one of us. I speak with many women who say with exasperation, "I don't know what my purpose in life is!" The idea that we're supposed to figure out this "purpose" can be stressful and cause fear . . . *What if I die before I figure out what my purpose is?*

It is easy to fall prey to the idea that other people have much more purpose than we do as the world defines it, especially if we live a day-to-day life that, from the world's perspective, doesn't seem to mean much. Our world speaks the lie that a life of purpose is one that is grand, one where you find acclaim and fame and money, one that affects the lives of dozens, hundreds, or thousands of people. This "purpose" must have a far-reaching ripple effect to mean anything at all.

The concept of purpose in God looks quite different.

A few years ago, Daniël and I took a road trip to Arizona for a conference. We made an eight-hour drive from Los Angeles to Tucson. The drive consists of seemingly endless miles of road and desert, sand extending as far as the eye can see. The only sights are old cacti and maybe a roadrunner or two scrambling across the flat land.

We stopped at a gas station in the middle of nowhere along the way. Maybe you've been to one of these gas stations, where you look at the person behind the counter in the little convenience store and think to yourself, *Where does this person live? There hasn't been civilization for miles!*

As Daniël filled the car with gas, I saw an older couple strug-gling to use the pump a few stalls over. I walked over to see what I could do. "Do you need help?" I asked. They began to respond in broken English, with an accent I knew well. I realized that they were Dutch.

What are the odds that I would find an elderly Dutch couple in the middle of the Arizona desert, stopped at this exact same gas station at this exact same moment, a place where my dear sweet Dutch husband could approach them and give them a moment of community and home by walking over and explaining something in their native language?

I walked back to Daniël and, smiling, said, "They're Dutch."

So, he approached the couple and to their shock began speak-ing in Dutch. They chatted joyfully, pumped their gas, and went on their way.

There was nothing grand about this exchange. Most people would label it a coincidence. But I do not believe there are coin-cidences in God . . . there is only purpose. There is purpose in all things in a life lived with the Lord.

Your heart is beating, you are breathing, you are awake and alive, and he has specific plans to use you in one million ways you cannot imagine, ways that perhaps are not grand or fanciful but that are packed with purpose—the kind of purpose that goes hand in hand with simple, humble service to Christ.

Perhaps it's the couple at the gas station. You step into the plan God had for you in that moment and live out his purpose for you to be there to give someone a moment of comfort and peace.

Maybe you had to give up your dreams to take care of your sick mother, who needs you. Your heart is beating, and he is using you, and there is purpose in this.

Maybe you are in medical school, battling against a culture of death and wondering if you should give it all up and go into a

profession where you don't feel so desperately alone in your beliefs. You are breathing, and his plan needs you, and there is purpose in this.

Maybe you get up all night with your baby, with other little ones tugging on you all day, inching ever closer to the point of breaking, wondering if God can really use you in the drudgery you feel your daily life has become. Blood is flowing through your veins, and God's will is unfolding within you, and there is purpose in this.

Maybe all the children God entrusted you to raise have spread their wings to fly, and you think your purpose has come to a close— and now it is rare for you to be needed or called upon by anyone. Your heartbeat is a sign that God has more in store for you. There is purpose in this.

When the flashy ideas of purpose the world clutters our minds with are stripped away, we are left with the reality that our purpose is one thing: To love and serve God in each moment of each day that he gives us here on earth.

This week is about reducing big-picture purpose to small-picture purpose—to zoom in and embrace the reality that there is purpose in the smallest things of today. It's about waking up to the truth that if you're moving and breathing, then God not only *can* use you today, but *wants* to use you today. As long as our hearts are beating, the purpose of that beating is service of the kingdom and of a King who gave his life so that we could wake up each day in gratitude and willingness to say, "Lord, there is purpose in this day. Lead me, guide me, and use me. I give my day, and my life, to be used for your will and for your glory. Amen."

SOUL EXERCISES

1. Recall a moment in your life when God clearly had a specific purpose for your whereabouts and actions. Reflect on the power of God in that moment and how he used you to do his will.
2. Set aside just five minutes each day this week to sit in quiet. Pay attention to your breathing and your heartbeat. Let it be a part of your prayer. As you pray in silence, what do you notice? Reflect on the reality that your heartbeat is a sure sign that God is not done using you to build his kingdom and pour out his love in the world.

YOUR HEART'S PRAYER
THIS WEEK

Jesus, I am so grateful to be alive. My heart is beating, and I am breathing. I praise you for the miracle that is my life. Thank you for creating me for a unique and beautiful purpose—the purpose only I can fulfill in this world. Help me to be faithful in the small and big pieces of living out this purpose, proclaiming a faithful yes to you in all things. I want to strive for greater obedience in following you wherever you lead me. Amen.

Week 25

Let People Love You

Years ago I was in South Africa preparing to play music at a night of worship in Johannesburg. I was drying my hair when the outlet converter malfunctioned (take my advice, just don't use a converter for a blow-dryer, ever, no matter how fancy it is; you'll save yourself a lot of trouble). The inside of the blow-dryer exploded all over me. It was one of the most frightening moments of my life.

Orange-hot coils went all over my chest and into my bra. They fell on the floor and immediately melted into the linoleum. It was terrifying. I was alone. There was no fire (thankfully!), but I immediately had some serious small circular wounds all over my chest.

I finished getting ready because I had no other choice, and debated for the rest of the day about whether or not I would tell anyone. My typical life approach was to just deal with it alone. *Don't trouble anyone; you shouldn't have been drying your hair anyway,* says my typical inner dialogue. So, for a whole day, I stayed quiet. But then the fear of infection began to creep in, and I was in pretty bad pain, so I decided that I had to say something. I told one of the people I had traveled with, who asked me to tell the head of the retreat center—and this person led me to an older nun who was a nurse. I felt silly and embarrassed for my stupidity, causing all this commotion and trouble.

I then had to meet with this old South African nun to show her the severity of my injury. I had to show her my chest as if to show her my heart and allow her to show me, a girl from America she had never met, the love of Christ in that moment.

This was very difficult because I find it hard to let myself be loved. I have never gotten to the root of why (admittedly, I probably haven't reflected on it long enough), but I really struggle to allow myself to be loved. When I was younger, I often wondered if I could open my heart up enough to ever get married. I definitely keep my guard up unnecessarily.

So, I ask you this week, Do you struggle to allow people to love you, too?

I created a poll once online. I asked all the women in my community this question: "If you receive help from people—support in some way, a listening ear, a favor—do you feel like you are burdening them?" A total of 5,678 women responded. Of these, 3,967 said yes; 1,711 said no.

I was shocked, both at the number of women who said yes and also at the knowledge that I am not alone in feeling this way. We can be reluctant to allow people to love us because we are afraid of getting hurt, or being let down, but we also don't allow people to love us because we fear we are a burden to them. I live with this fear every day—and it is not of the Lord. My mom drove an hour and a half to my house so that she could watch the baby while I packed before a move. I felt overwhelming guilt the entirety of her stay, even though she was happy to love me in this way. I would be happy to do anything for her at any time, and I know that is the way she feels about me, but it can be hard to conquer the fear of being a bothersome inconvenience.

I have learned much from Zion in this way. He has a completely unencumbered acceptance of my love. He soaks it all in and doesn't even understand what the word *burden* means—so there's no space in his heart to think, *Wow, by crying every two hours in the night, I'm really burdening my mom!* He accepts all the love I give him—every last ounce of the love I pour out to him every day.

Some of us resist love because we think we are too messy. Maybe you think that if you let someone in, they'll see who you really are and be disgusted or turned off by your imperfections and your mess. Authentic love sees the mess and stays. It's the love from someone who says, "Yes, I see who you are. I see that you are not perfect. I am not perfect either, and I choose to love you. I want you to open your heart to receive that love rather than push me away. I want to go out of my way for you because I love you."

If you struggle to accept love, this is the week to dig into the why, to ask yourself, "Why is this sometimes so difficult for me?"

This is the week to look at opening yourself in a new way to the love of God, who sees the mess and stays. This is the week to pray for a greater openness to the ways that the people in your life want to love you. This is the week to say, "Lord, give me the grace to allow people to love me and to see the love I've been shown as a reflection of your face, of your love, of your heart. Amen."

SOUL EXERCISE

Can you recall a moment when you were made to feel like a burden, or a time when you first began to struggle to let people love you? Take the time to enter into a prayer exercise with Jesus about this moment.

- ❤ Invite Jesus into this memory. Ask him to heal your heart and undo any damage caused by your feelings of being rejected, unwanted, lonely, or unlovable.
- ❤ If you recall a person who made you feel this way, offer a prayer for that person. Ask Jesus to heal any wounds they may harbor that caused them to hurt you, either intentionally or unintentionally.

YOUR HEART'S PRAYER THIS WEEK

Jesus, help me to let go of my fear of being an annoyance, an inconvenience, or a burden to people. I want to let myself be loved. I want to believe the truth that I am lovable. I want to open my heart to the reality that there are people in my life who love me for who I am. Heal my memories of times

I was made to feel like a burden for struggling, for needing help, or for simply existing. I desire freedom from this fear. Please grant it to me! Amen.

**Week
26**

Ask Jesus Who
You Are

During World War II, countless people were displaced from their homes. Some were imprisoned in concentration camps, many left to fight in the war, and some moved away to safer lands. The chaos of life when it all ended was immense. Among those displaced were many French soldiers with amnesia. Because of trauma and other factors, these soldiers came out of the war without any recollection of who they were, where they had come from, or even what their name was. Their memories had been completely erased. Someone had the idea to hold an event at the Paris Opera House with the goal of reuniting these men with their families.

The plan was to invite anyone searching for loved ones to the theater for the night, and allow the soldiers to stand on the stage in front of the audience in hopes that someone would know who they were. I imagine many people shuffling into the theater that evening, eager to see their husband or child or brother but trying not to get their hopes too high. These people already knew devastation beyond what we will ever be able to comprehend.

The time came for each soldier to step into the lights. As the story goes, one of the men came forward as everyone held their breath. He walked to the front of the stage in this historic theater and shouted in French into the darkness of the crowd, "Does anybody know who I am?"

I get chills thinking of him shouting out that question in hopes that someone, anyone, would know his story . . . would know his heart . . . would simply know his name. I wish I could tell you how this man's story ended, but I don't have that information. I do know that this story offers a heartbreaking yet poignant analogy for our search for identity today.

"Does anybody know who I am?" Is this not a question that many of us ask, subconsciously or with our actions? Is this not a search we all share—the search for identity, for someone to know us so deeply and intimately that if we stood before a crowd, they would exclaim our name with surety and joy? We are in a crisis of identity

because we place our identity in so many things—our work, our social media accounts, our achievements, our relationships.

I have shared a simple prayer with many of you that has been so important to my life—and this week is about that prayer. *Jesus, tell me who I am.*

I invite you to sit with that prayer long and hard this week. It is likely that people around you have spoken to you of who you are—and some of those things have been true, but some of them have been false. Some people have spoken lies to you about your identity residing in what you do instead of who you are. Some people have spoken mistruths to you about your intelligence, your capabilities, your worth. It is the simplest prayer, and the answers the Lord speaks can wipe away the falsehoods and all the other clutter that keeps us from being rooted in him.

Jesus, tell me who I am.

I often invite women at conferences and retreats to earnestly pray that prayer to the Lord. In speaking with women after these events, I ask how God responded to them. One woman said that when she asked the Lord to tell her who she is, the Lord replied, quietly and gently, "Sandy."

Her name was Sandra, and she had not been called by this nickname since she was very small. She knew in an instant that the Lord was speaking to her as she is to him—a little girl, full of freedom and joy and possibility. That is the beauty of sitting with this prayer—the Lord may speak to you in an image, or in a thought, perhaps with a name, or a word. I invite you to sit in that place. Sit with the truth that the Lord speaks to you of who you are and who he created you to be. Don't rush it. Take time for this prayer every day—even if just for five minutes. Lean into the truth the Lord speaks, and let it wash away the lies you have been told.

As you sit with God this week, embrace how *known* you really are. There is power in someone knowing you and who you are . . .

especially when you cannot remember yourself. Allow yourself to hear Jesus speak your name with joy and knowledge of you.

He knows who you are. He knows where you've been. He knows where you're going.

Jesus, tell me who I am.

Sit with him this week and listen to the answer. I think it will bring you joy.

SOUL EXERCISES

1. Have you ever felt like that soldier standing on the edge of the stage, searching for who you are—*whose* you are? Imagine God's response. Feel his Fatherly embrace enveloping you, and take in his unwavering love.
2. *Jesus, tell me who I am.* Sit with that prayer, even for a short while, every day, and truly listen. Don't overlook the places he wants to take you in this prayer with him.

YOUR HEART'S PRAYER THIS WEEK

Oh Jesus, I root my identity and self-esteem in so many sources. Whether it is my work, academics, my relationship status, the opinions of others, the number on the scale, or something else, I get lost in the confusion of who I am. Open my ears to hear the truth that you speak of my identity. Remind me in my moments of searching that who I am will always be anchored in you and your Sacred Heart. Amen.

Week 27

Give Thanks to the Lord

I don't know about you, but I have a long list of first-world problems. (If you are unfamiliar with that term, it refers to relatively trivial or minor problems compared with the difficulties experienced by those in the developing world.) We all have first-world problems. We experience frustration when the Wi-Fi is too slow, annoyance when the coffee machine at work is broken, exasperation when we have to wait in a long line at the grocery store with our full shopping cart.

I recall a first-world frustration I experienced a few years ago. It's embarrassing to admit it, but one day I thought to myself, *I cannot believe that I have to keep taking showers for the rest of my life.* At the time, I was single and exercising a lot and had plenty of time to take care of myself. For some reason, having to shower seemed like a nuisance to me. Now that I'm a mother, my shower is the most treasured part of my day aside from my prayer time with the Lord. It is my oasis, my refreshment, and such a gift to me in the midst of the craziness that is motherhood!

When I realized that I was frustrated with the necessity of showering until my dying day, I was disgusted. I thought to myself, *Do you know how fortunate you are that you can take a hot shower every day?*

I am always surprised when I pass the bottled-water section at Costco. It costs just $2.99 for twenty-four bottles of clean, pure, perfect water. If I so desire, I can hoist that big package into my cart, take it home in the car, and drink all of it without another thought. I don't consider what a blessing this is. During the end of my pregnancy with Zion, I craved ice, and lots of it. Daniël would stop at the store every day to get me a big cup of crushed ice (not cubed). I have clean water—and beyond that, I have the luxury of choosing what type of ice I want at any moment!

I suppose that, like me, you take clean, safe water for granted. When was the last time you took a revitalizing shower and thought, *Wow, what a gift!* When was the last time you washed your hands,

drank from the water fountain at school, filled your Hydro Flask, or washed plates in your sink and thought, *Wow, what a gift!*

We cannot overestimate the value of good, clean water. In poor countries all over the world, people walk for hours each day to obtain clean water for their families. Women carry buckets on their heads, balancing them in the hot sun so that their families can drink and wash. Unsafe water is a main cause of illness and death among hundreds of thousands of people. One billion people in developing countries have no access to clean water.

And here I am complaining about what a nuisance it is to shower with clean, hot water for the rest of my life.

This week is about a shift toward gratitude. This week is about giving thanks for every drop of water I use and offering a prayer for those who would give so much for a hot shower, for clean water to give their babies, for a piece of ice to cool their mouths in the heat of the day—whether those people are homeless in your city or mothers in Africa. This week, as you turn on the shower, I invite you to pray, *Thank you, Lord.* As you press the start button on your washing machine or dishwasher, fill up the water side of your Keurig, or wash your hands, I invite you to fervently say it out loud: *Thank you, Lord.*

Clean water is an incomparable blessing, if we only have the eyes to see.

SOUL EXERCISES

1. Be intentionally aware of every time you use clean water this week and say an audible thanks to God, even if you are with other people. Share about your exercise of gratitude if they ask.
2. Take a little time this week to research the water crisis in the world, and think about how you can be part of the solution.

YOUR HEART'S PRAYER THIS WEEK

Jesus, awaken my heart to how blessed I am to have clean water to drink, to shower and cook with, and to provide to my family. What a gift that I have taken for granted for so long! May I never take it for granted again. Amen.

Week
28

Get It Done

Confession time: I'm a procrastinator. I won't try to hide it. I am typically the person who sends things in *juuuuuust* before the deadline, cutting it super close because I've waited until the final minute. I am superb at daydreaming all day long about how to change the world, but getting things organized and complete is not my strong suit. When I was a teenager, however, there was one day every year when I deliberately chose to do things very differently.

In high school, on the day when school was dismissed for Christmas vacation, I would go home and that very evening sit down and do all the homework I had been assigned for the entire vacation. I completed all of it—every assignment from each one of my seven classes—and it took many hours, but I wanted to enjoy my time off from school. I didn't want to spend the last day of my vacation frantically trying to finish papers. I wanted to relax. I didn't want the dark cloud of essays and reading and worksheets hanging over my Christmas cheer and my eggnog and my caroling.

And sure enough, when I graduated from high school, I realized there was a method to the madness in my self-imposed Christmas vacation homework policy.

Since then, I have come to see that procrastinating is a surefire way to prevent myself from truly enjoying life or having time for what is important. I cannot live well and peacefully when I am constantly running behind and late to everything. I cannot carve out time to spend in prayer with Jesus. I cannot keep up with everything that needs to be done, because I'm wasting my time on mindless, unimportant things. I decided after many years of procrastination that I did not want to live this way anymore.

Maybe you live this way, too, and you're as tired of it as I am. You might think, *Well, I can't just* choose *not to procrastinate.* As a matter of fact, that's actually all it takes. All it takes is a choice.

I read a trendy little Pinterest quote that said, "If you're not changing it, you're choosing it," which applies perfectly here. We choose to start getting ready three minutes before we are supposed

to be out the door. We choose to watch Netflix when we've been given three weeks to write a paper, and then wait to start it the day before it's due. We choose to spend hours scrolling social media and give just a few moments to God as we fall asleep. Procrastination prevents us from living a properly ordered life. Constant procrastination keeps us from prioritizing things properly. We let our prayer time fall to the wayside, put investment in friendships or marriage on the back burner, and find ourselves constantly scrambling to keep up. A life of procrastination will not lead to peace. It will not allow time for true intimacy with Christ. Instead it will leave things disorganized and out of order.

I challenge you to spend this week following my Christmas vacation policy. Whether that means completing your assignments, meeting your deadlines, finishing a project, folding the laundry, emptying the trash, making a phone call, or scheduling an appointment, just *get it done.*

Do it immediately and make space for God. Complete the to-do list and make time for true rest. Get it done so you can live an ordered life with a peaceful heart.

SOUL EXERCISES

1. Do you put off doing chores around the house? This week, when something needs to be done (the trash taken out, the dishwasher emptied, your bed made), and you are able in that moment (given your circumstances with children, etc.), do it immediately.

2. Do you procrastinate by watching TV or scrolling through social media? This week, create a schedule for necessary tasks and activities, including solid prayer time, putting your life in proper order. You can do enjoyable extras after you have completed those activities.

YOUR HEART'S PRAYER
THIS WEEK

Jesus, my tendency to procrastinate can really bog me down. I desire a life that is ordered, with my priorities in proper place, and I need your assistance in creating an ordered life. Help me to be disciplined in completing tasks so that I may live in peace, with time and space for you, my true and first priority. Amen.

Week 29

Love the Elderly

Do not cast me aside in my
old age; as my strength fails,
do not forsake me.

—Psalm 71:9

I still remember the distinct scent of a particular brand of women's powder that would come like a cloud in the sky every Tuesday. When I was growing up, I went to a Catholic elementary school, and every Tuesday morning, the senior citizens' club, delightfully named the Happy Times Club, would meet in the parish hall on our campus. Dozens of seniors would come and enjoy this time playing games and eating lunch together and celebrating holidays.

Not until I had more life experience did I realize that these few hours were probably the highlight of the week for many of them. Not until I had more life experience and spoke with wise and wonderful older people did I realize how lonely it can be to grow old.

A woman I spoke to revealed to me the importance of caring for the elderly. She explained that a deteriorating body is difficult to deal with, a deteriorating mind even more so, but that the real pain of getting old is that all your friends start to die. This had never occurred to me.

I've had friends move away. Leaving my friends to go to college was hard. It's difficult to maintain friendships as a mother. But I had never thought about the sad reality that as an elderly person, your friends have not simply moved away—one by one, they move on to meet God. And during this season of their lives, the elderly, some of whom go through months when life seems like one funeral after another, need to be visited, called, and loved with the love of Christ—and you and I can do just that.

My dear grandmother was homebound for the last years of her life and lived on the opposite coast from me. The main connections she had to the outside world were the Internet and the phone. I called her every once in a while, but now that she has passed away, I realize how much more often I should have called—how just a few minutes every few days would have been a small but powerful exercise in the love of Christ and intentionally loving her in her old age. I regret not calling more.

We moved into our first home about six months ago. I soon noticed that an elderly woman lived directly behind us, and I often saw her sitting on her couch alone, looking out her living room window. When Zion and I looked out the window of his nursery each night before bed, I saw her sitting in the exact same spot on the end of her couch. I imagined she would enjoy having a visitor and intended to go over to introduce ourselves, but I kept putting it off because of the busyness of life. Just a few weeks ago, the curtains to that living room window were closed for the first time, and I knew immediately in my heart that she was no longer there. Those curtains had never once been closed in the months since we moved in. I do not know if she has passed away or if she was moved into an assisted-living home, but I do know this—it is too late for me to show her the love of Christ, and I regret it very much. Yesterday I saw workers staging her home with furniture before it goes up for sale, and I thought of the opportunity that Christ had given me to reach out to this woman. I am ashamed that I did not carve out the time and, by not doing so, said no to an opportunity to love abundantly.

When I am out in public with my son, older people make comments about him often. I make a point to stop for a while and talk, sometimes longer than I have time for, because there is no way to know how lonely these people are and how badly they need a chat and a little hand-hold from a cute baby for a brief time. A little conversation goes a long way in the ache of loneliness or longing for companionship. One phone call or visit to your grandfather can make a big impact on his week. One conversation with an older woman at church—a compliment on her dress or a sincere "How are you doing?" and listening attentively to her answer, instead of walking out the door as soon as church is over, trying not to make eye contact with anyone—can represent the hands and feet of Christ much more than we realize.

As much as you and I need reminders that we are seen, known, and loved, the elderly around us do, too. They need to know they are not forgotten, and you can be the person who, even just for a moment, sees them this week. Do not, like me, wait until it's too late. Reach out and love abundantly today.

SOUL EXERCISES

1. This week, take some time to pray for your grandparents, whether they have passed away or are still living. If they are still living, consider a concrete way you can show them the love of Christ—whether through a visit, a phone call, or another gesture.
2. Be attentive this week to the elderly people you may encounter in your daily routine. Make the extra effort to begin a conversation with them, ask them a thoughtful question, or engage with them in some other kindhearted way.

YOUR HEART'S PRAYER THIS WEEK

Jesus, awaken my heart to the love I can show to the elderly souls in my life. Help me to open my heart to their needs, their sorrows, and the ways I can love them as you love them. May I be a light to show them that they are not forgotten, they are not cast aside, but they are loved by you and so many others. Amen.

Week 30

Give It Over to God

Change. Transition. New phases. It all terrifies me. The unknown is often very difficult and scary for me. I cried my eyes out the night before I started high school in sadness over finishing elementary school; as I have shared with you, I spent some time during my engagement fearful of the unknown of getting married; and there are many other moments in my life when I've been troubled by the loss of a routine, scene, identity, or home that I had grown accustomed to calling my own. All the change has worked out better than I anticipated, but the act of letting go of things, people, the past—and moving on to new things—is always raw and difficult for me.

In the movie *Life of Pi*, the main character states, "I suppose in the end, the whole of life becomes an act of letting go, but what always hurts the most is not taking a moment to say goodbye." That line struck me to my core. I realized that yes, as we grow older, life does become so much about letting go of things and moving into new adventures—and that can be a process we try to avoid. We don't want to say goodbye. We don't want to let go.

About eight years ago, I led my first four-day retreat. It was exhausting (I slept for *seventeen* hours on the night I returned home!), and at the time I was working at my my first real job out of college, teaching school, so it was a *big* life change for me. At the end of the retreat, everyone gathered together for a big closing ceremony with lots of tears and hugging and fanfare. When it was over, I unloaded all the retreat supplies at my office and got in my car to leave. I suddenly experienced an overwhelming feeling of nostalgia in my heart . . . and I started driving, not wanting to head home but not really knowing where to go.

I ended up at my childhood home somehow. I had no idea why I drove there. But I parked my white 2000 Toyota Avalon outside that beautiful house with the wraparound driveway and big glass front window, and I cried my eyes out. I didn't understand at the time why I was crying so much, but in the years since I have come to see that sitting there on the street crying was, for me, an act of

letting go. Along with the big life change of entering my first "real" job, I realized that some part of me had to accept my adulthood and the fact that I was now out on my own, responsible for taking care of myself, managing finances, and all the other big, little, and incredibly overwhelming things that come along with adulthood. It was painful for me to acknowledge that I was not a child anymore, to embrace the fact that that season was over and that I was now a part of the adult world.

In that moment, I had an experience of letting go and surrendering to God what had been—and surrendering to him my uncertainty about what was to come. That was a significant release for me, and in light of this reflection I ask you, What do you need to let go? Maybe there is an answer that bubbles up quickly in your heart. Maybe it requires a bit more thought. Maybe it's the marriage you had planned on with your ex-boyfriend. Maybe it's acceptance into your dream school. Maybe it's the way your labor and delivery turned out. Maybe it's a regret you've been holding on to for too long.

Sometimes we come to places in our lives when we must face the loss of things we did not ever anticipate losing. Sometimes that's a friendship, sometimes that's our childhood, sometimes that is an event we wanted to happen but that we need to accept never will. In the process of grieving, we can surrender these things to God. Grieving is a necessary, difficult, yet beautiful process of experiencing our emotions, of entering into sadness with Christ present to us all the while, and of handing that which we grieve over to his gentle, loving care. When we let go of pain and grief in the light of faith, Christ can make beautiful things emerge. He can make beauty from ashes and magnificence from our messes, if we allow him.

All grieving requires letting go, and sometimes that must be a tangible act. Driving to my childhood home. Taking down the instructions on the fridge my husband wrote for when I would go into labor after things went much differently than expected.

Deleting a phone number. Getting rid of an ex-boyfriend's sweater or removing his photos from your accounts.

It is easy to glide over these things as we do them, or to never do them at all, moving on as quickly as we can and never taking the step to feel the pain and then hand that pain over to the Lord. It is easier to just skate by in life than to take the time to reflect in the moving on. It is easier to hang on to that sweater or to keep the phone number because it keeps the door open for *maybe*.

The Lord is inviting you into something new this week. He beckons you into the freedom that comes with saying goodbye to the things we cling tightly to so he can lead us to new places with unhindered hearts.

What do you need to let go of? How can you free your heart from what it is holding on to? Are there actions you need to take this week to move on from "maybe" and to sever ties with what God has revealed is not supposed to be? It is time. With God by your side, present to the pain that comes with the letting go and saying goodbye, you have all the courage you need.

Say goodbye in the letting go and greet what is to come with open arms.

SOUL EXERCISE

Take time this week to identify the sources of baggage in your life. Maybe you need to stop following someone on social media, or you need to give away an item that reminds you of someone from the past. Figure out what triggers thoughts about the past and say goodbye to those things—either in your heart and through prayer, or by actually throwing away an item or ceasing your visits to a certain place.

YOUR HEART'S PRAYER THIS WEEK

Jesus, sometimes I struggle to move on from past events. This week, I pray for the courage to let go. Give me the courage and freedom to say goodbye to whatever I am holding on to that keeps me from the present, keeps me from true joy, keeps me from you. Awaken my heart to whatever inhibits me from moving on, moving forward, and carrying on with this life. Amen.

**Week
31**

Bring Down the Walls

Some allergies are present the day a person is born, and some allergies develop over time. I have been sensitive to dust and pollen for my entire life. However, when I had a baby, I suddenly became allergic to bananas and Pantene Pro-V conditioner. I am not sure how this happens—how you can be just fine eating bananas one year and then the next year eating a banana causes you so much pain you can barely stand up. But I'm not going to ask you to spend this week reflecting on my mysterious allergy to bananas. Rather, let's talk about an allergy that every one of us has: vulnerability.

We are allergic to being vulnerable.

It's not an allergy we are born with, but an aversion that slowly manifests in our hearts over time. Children are quite good at exercising vulnerability—they will share openly about how they are feeling and what is going on in their lives. They may even share private information with strangers, leaving their mother or father horrified that what they said at home spilled out of their child's mouth in the grocery store. Our willingness to share seems to diminish as we mature. As we gain a greater understanding of privacy, we become less willing to open our hearts to others.

Why? As we grow up, we become close to people and share meaningful or private things with them, but soon find out that not everyone can be trusted with our thoughts and feelings. When those we confide in break our trust and reveal those private, tender things to others, we get hurt. And that makes us less willing to be vulnerable with someone else the next time we are given an opportunity.

When we are trusting and vulnerable, and that trust is broken, we think, *Well, if I'm never vulnerable again with anyone, they won't be able to hurt me. If I don't give people the opportunity to break my trust, they never will!*

So, we snap closed like a clam. We just shut up and shut off, and sometimes we start building. We build little walls around our hearts to keep people out so they can't hurt us, can't use things against us,

can't see inside to what's really going on in our hearts and souls and lives . . . and we're thinking, *Woo-hoo, I'm safe here!*

But that feeling of safety starts to fade over time, and we become miserable. Instead of feeling secure inside our walls, we feel sad and lonely—for good reason. We were made for intimate relationship. We were made in the image and likeness of God, and God is Trinity—Father, Son, and Holy Spirit—three persons in relationship in one. We crave this relationship. We crave closeness with people. Whether I want to admit it or not, I desire deeply to be seen and known and loved for who I really am. I desire to let people in. I want to be vulnerable. We all do.

But that requires effort and work.

I am not asking you to suddenly start sharing with everyone. I am not inviting you to attempt to take down all the walls you've built up with one swing of the sledgehammer. But some of our walls are so thick, so tall, so wide, that even an army would have trouble getting through, and this is a recipe for a superficial life.

If we do not allow ourselves to be vulnerable with people who are close to us, we will never experience the depths of love that relationships and friendships can reach. We will never grasp the reality of relationship that Christ calls us to—to share deeply in life with one another in a way that goes far beyond the surface and drills into the depths and messiness of the human experience.

Sometimes being vulnerable means asking for help when you need it. Sometimes being vulnerable means sharing a piece of your past that is difficult to bring up or makes you feel ashamed. Sometimes being vulnerable means opening your heart to the possibility of being hurt and rejected. Sometimes being vulnerable means telling a friend simply, "I would love to become better friends with you."

I invite you this week to take a reflective look at the walls that you've built around yourself and to ask Jesus to help you take them down, brick by brick. Allow him to show you the places where the

walls must come down for you to live a life of true connection, filled with beautiful relationships and reflective of the Most Holy Trinity.

SOUL EXERCISES

1. What comes to mind when you think about being vulnerable with others? Is there any hesitation or hardening of your heart?
2. Recall a moment when your trust was betrayed and you started building walls to protect yourself. Invite Jesus to heal that memory and to show you his grace in the present.
3. Brené Brown says, "Vulnerability connects hearts." Is there a time when this has been true in your life? A time when you allowed yourself to be open and you were surprised by how your openness connected you with another person?

YOUR HEART'S PRAYER THIS WEEK

Jesus, I know you did not create me to live a life spent behind walls that keep others out. You created me for a life reflective of the Trinity, of true connection and relationship with others. Help me to bring down the walls I have built around my heart so that I can trust others fully and be open with the reliable people in my life. Heal the places of my heart that have been scarred by rejection and betrayal so that I can learn to fully trust again. Please bring people into

my life whom I can trust in meaningful and lasting friendship. And most importantly, Jesus, give me the courage to be vulnerable with you. Amen.

Week 32

Notice the Blooms

Notice how the flowers grow.
They do not toil or spin.
—Luke 12:27

I think one of the sweetest sights in the world is a man carrying a bouquet of flowers. They could be for his mother, wife, girlfriend, daughter, or sister—I never know who they are for, but when I see a man with a bouquet, I want to high-five him for his thoughtfulness.

Near the entrance to our grocery store lies the flower department, but I only notice it when I see a thoughtful man there perusing his many flower options. I usually make a quick turn toward the produce section, missing the opportunity to stop for even a few seconds to admire the beauty of God's design in that one simple thing—a flower.

My husband likes to buy me orchids. I love orchids. I just haven't figured out how to keep them alive. From what I hear, I'm not alone. Orchids are a wee bit high-maintenance. Daniël buys them for me, maybe four orchid plants a year, but I can't seem to get it right. "Ice cubes," my aunt told me, "two per week." The little brochure that comes with the orchid says how much light my little flower needs, but somehow they don't thrive. All I know how to do well is enjoy my orchids while they last.

I take a walk with Zion almost every day. We call it our nature walk because he likes to reach out and touch little plants and flowers, to feel them with his tiny hands and look at them closely. We watch spiders building their webs and lizards running across the pavement. He loves it. I lived in our townhome complex for three years before Zion was born, but it wasn't until we began our nature walks that I noticed the beautiful yellow lilies that grow along one row of houses. There are dozens of brilliant canary yellow lilies, and I never once noticed them. On one of our nature walks, Zion started waving and pointing at them so that I could roll him over in his stroller to feel their petals. I was unaware of them until my son forced me to slow down and see.

I am always amazed by the beauty of flowers—most especially their colors. The bright fuchsia of a bougainvillea. The rich yellow of the lilies near our home. The deep crimson of roses. The bright

red of the poinsettias that fill our church during Christmastime. How often do I stop to say, "*Wow!*"?

When was the last time you stopped to examine the intricate design of a flower? When was the last time you walked by a rose and paused to breathe it in?

This week is simple . . . it is about literally stopping to take in the flowers, because Jesus tells us in plain language to notice the flowers. I imagine you will run across at least a bloom or two this week. Perhaps it is springtime and there are flowers *everywhere*. Take time to appreciate their beauty this week. Look at them, feel them, and breathe in their fragrance. As carefully as the Lord crafts each flower, he crafted you and me. Flowers tell the story of God's thoughtful design, his loving attention, to them and to you and me.

"How varied are your works, LORD! In wisdom you have made them all; the earth is full of your creatures" (Ps 104:24).

SOUL EXERCISES

1. Bring flowers to someone this week. Maybe one, maybe a bouquet. Surprise someone with the joy and beauty that the gift of flowers can bring.
2. Pay close attention to the flowers you see this week. Think of the Lord and his creativity as you observe each one. As carefully and thoughtfully as he designed each of these, he designed *you*. Amazing.

YOUR HEART'S PRAYER
THIS WEEK

Jesus, how wonderful are your works! I thank you with a full heart for the dazzling hues and the sweet fragrances of the flowers that surround me. Help me to notice your creativity more. Help me to comprehend your careful artistry and appreciate the beauty it adds to my life. Amen.

**Week
33**

Claim a Legacy
of Love

My nana passed away eleven months before my son was born, and it will always be hard for me that she didn't get to meet him. Most people love babies, but Nana *loved* babies. She was homebound with illness during the last few years of her life, and oh, how I would have loved to send her pictures of my baby as she sat at home. I know she would have been thrilled to receive a photo every thirty minutes—no quantity of messages would have been overkill. There is much that I would give to have had her meet my son.

Sometimes we feel that we shouldn't "still" be sad about people we love who have passed away. Nana has been gone three years now, and it is still hard. I still cry when Frank Sinatra's voice comes crooning over the car radio or in a coffee shop. I immediately picture her sitting next to me belting out the lyrics without a care in the world, and I'm reminded of the closeness we shared.

I imagine you have lost someone you love, too. It's hard to not be able to call them, to not be able to share what's going on in our lives with them. Death can be painful and confusing, especially when people we love live a relatively short life.

As a teenager, I had two mentors, Mrs. Cirelle and Mrs. Nick. Mrs. Cirelle was one of my elementary school teachers, a wonderful wife and mother and a woman of strong faith. She was my sponsor for the sacrament of Confirmation, which means she helped me prepare to receive the sacrament and was charged with fostering my faith. A year after my Confirmation, her husband got very sick and died. Not long after, Mrs. Cirelle found out she had brain cancer and soon passed away. They were both in their fifties. I did not understand why God took her home at her age. I did not understand why I had to lose the first person I considered my mentor only two years after we had begun a relationship. I couldn't travel home for the funeral, so at times I feel as if I never got to say goodbye.

A few years later, God brought a new mentor into my life, Mrs. Nick. If you've ever read my writings, you've probably heard her

name. She was the director of campus ministry at my high school. I did not know her well when I was a student there, but she encouraged me to apply to be her assistant in 2011. I got the job and worked alongside her, learning from the depths of her passionate heart the desire for women to know their worth. A year into our time together, she was diagnosed with a relapse of the cancer that she had beat a few years earlier, and soon after that, she went home to meet God.

After I met Daniël, I visited Mrs. Nick as she lay sick on the hospital bed in her home. I don't know how I found the courage to bring it up, but I said I was going back to Europe because I had met a good man. I showed her a photo of Daniël, and I saw her heart light up. She said, "Don't be afraid to fall in love." It was the last thing she would ever tell me.

I was on stage at a conference in Kansas when my phone rang, and Mrs. Nick's name flashed across the screen. *Maybe she's feeling better*, I thought to myself. *Oh, glory, maybe she's feeling better.* I returned her call only to find out that she was, at that moment, reveling in the glory of God at the heavenly gates. Her husband answered the phone and lovingly told me she had gone home to him. I stood on the lawn at Benedictine College, the humidity of the day soaking my skin, and once again felt the loss of a mentor in my faith just two years after our friendship began.

I had to give a talk that night. It was my first big keynote talk, and I wondered how I would say anything after hearing that my mentor had just died. It was a flurry of an afternoon, but that night, when I began to talk about St. Joan of Arc and the surrender she modeled by her life, there was an electricity in my blood that I had not known before. I realized that night that my mission was to do the work that God had planned for me and to carry on Mrs. Nick's legacy of work with young women.

There is something we can do when the people we love have passed away. We can carry on their love in the world, we can carry

on what they have taught us, we can carry on what they showed us by their lives.

Nana taught me to stop and smell the roses. Mrs. Cirelle taught me to be steadfast, even in the midst of deep suffering. Mrs. Nick taught me to pour out my heart for young women until I feel as though I can't pour out anymore, and then to just keep pouring. What have the people you love who have passed away taught you?

This week I invite you to think about the legacy left by the people you love, and to reflect on how you are living out that legacy. What did they teach you? What did you admire about the way they lived? How can you carry on their legacy? Perhaps it's a legacy of compassion, of generosity, of listening, of faith. It's up to us to say, *I will carry the light, the love, the goodness they shared with me to every person I meet . . . I will pray for their soul and pour water on the seeds they planted in my heart during their life.* This is a week to call a friend or family member who knew your loved one and simply talk about them . . . the things you miss, shared memories, what you are struggling with in their absence. This is a week to reflect on the truth that it is not only okay but good to miss the people we love. And we can ask the Lord to be present in our grief, to comfort us, and to give us the fortitude to carry on their legacy.

SOUL EXERCISE

Take time to journal about the people you love who have passed away. What did they teach you? What do you want to carry on as their legacy in the world?

YOUR HEART'S PRAYER
THIS WEEK

Jesus, thank you for the loved ones in my life who have passed away. Help me to keep their memory alive by living what they taught me—by sharing the faith, hope, and love they gave me and the world. Help me to rest and trust in the reality that you conquered death—that by your death and Resurrection, you unlocked the doors to eternal life. I lift up the souls of my loved ones to you; may they rest in the light of your face and in your glory forever. Amen.

Week
34

Rest Close to His Heart

St. Faustina was a Polish nun who recorded very personal conversations she had with the Lord for the last few years of her life. Eventually, her diary was made public (as the Lord requested of her in prayer). This is one of my favorite lines in the whole of her writings:

"My daughter, rest close to my heart. Known to me are your efforts."

I believe that the Lord wants to tell every woman this same message: "I know your efforts." He sees what you do. He sees every last detail of the service and generosity you pour into the world. Nothing goes unnoticed by him.

Sometimes, this knowledge does not feel like enough. In our humanity, we want attention and affirmation for the hard work we do. It stings when you work on a project for weeks only to have your boss say nothing or fail to recognize your great effort. It's hard when you devote hundreds of hours to volunteering at your parish and no one bothers to thank you for what you have contributed. It's difficult to tend to your children day in and day out without anyone to say, "Hey, you are raising those children very generously. Great job!" You may not be recognized for the arduous effort to live chastely in a relationship, to make good choices in dating, or to resist the temptation of a certain sin. It can be hard to devote yourself to caring

for a sick family member, to give up your personal dreams to help your family, and have that sacrifice go unappreciated. I have seen women get in bitter fights over one woman's belief that she went unnoticed for her hard work on some event, in some ministry. It is a normal craving of our human hearts to want someone to see and say, "Good work. Great job. I see what you are doing."

Enter humility.

The virtue of humility asks us to surrender this longing to the Lord and let him pierce our hearts again and again with the truth that the only thing that matters is him seeing it all. He knows. He is watching. He is listening.

The virtue of humility accepts that this is enough. Pride alone causes us to seek recognition and acclaim. It is the voice of pride in our hearts that says, *People should be thanking me for all of this. People should notice how much I'm giving. These people who don't care are self-centered and unappreciative.* When we strive for humility, we can allow the words of Christ—"I know your efforts"—to wash over all of the affirmation and applause we seek for gritty giving and sacrificial pouring out. Humility asks us to step back and know that our all-knowing God notices it all, and that is all that will ever really matter.

If you identify this desire to be recognized for what you do, or feel overlooked and unappreciated, sit with that line from Faustina's diary this week. Surrender this human desire to the Lord, asking him to give you the grace to serve and keep serving, knowing that God's presence and love in the midst of our efforts is the greatest reward of all.

"Nor, indeed, did we ever appear with flattering speech, as you know, or with a pretext for greed—God is witness—nor did we seek praise from human beings, either from you or from others, although we were able to impose our weight as apostles of Christ" (1 Thes 2:5–7).

SOUL EXERCISES

1. How can you practice more humility? Where can you allow these words from the Lord—"I see your efforts"—to comfort you in your own life, as they did for St. Faustina?

2. Ponder these select lines from the Litany of Humility, and choose one to focus on this week:

   ♥ From the desire of being esteemed, *deliver me, O Jesus.*

   ♥ From the desire of being praised, *deliver me, O Jesus.*

   ♥ That others may be esteemed more than I, *Jesus, grant me the grace to desire it.*

   ♥ That others may be praised and I go unnoticed, *Jesus, grant me the grace to desire it.*

YOUR HEART'S PRAYER THIS WEEK

Jesus, thank you for seeing the efforts I make to serve and love you with my life. Today, I give you any pain or resentment that has taken up residence in my heart. I choose to let go of my pride and walk in humility in all things, living a life of humble service,

dedicated to your mission and your heart. I will rest close to your heart knowing that you see and you know, trusting in faith that on the day when I see you face-to-face, I will hear those most beautiful words, "Well done, my good and faithful servant." Amen.

Week 35

Thank God for Good Friends

What a great favor God does to
those he places in the company
of good people.
—St. Teresa of Avila

Authentic friendship and community are wonderful gifts and great blessings in life. Deep, meaningful friendships can awaken our hearts to the voice and love of God in our lives. When you hear or read the word *friendship*, do you feel joy and security? Or does the word make you pause because you do not feel you have many friends, if even a friend at all? Friendship can be a difficult aspect of life for women, one that takes much care and attention, especially in the midst of hectic lives.

No matter how many good friendships you may have, one thing is true: Each friendship is a gift, each friend a reflection of the love of God and a person we can bring toward Christ.

One of the most wonderful passages in scripture about true friendship is often overlooked—the story of the four men and their paralytic friend (Mk 2). When these men hear that Jesus has returned to Capernaum, they bring their paralytic friend to the house where he is staying. The house is so packed with people that there is no room for them to get him through the door and close to Jesus, so they climb onto the roof and *break through* (it says those exact words in scripture!) the roof to lower him in. (The scripture makes no mention of how the owner of the house felt about this!) Which of your friends would break through a roof to make sure you got to Jesus in a time of need? Which of your friends make certain as the months go on that they are leading you to Christ and not away from him? Which of your friends have been there for you in thick and thin, in times of great need?

And as you call to mind those friends, I also ask, when was the last time thanks overflowed from your heart to the ears of Christ for bringing these people into your life?

Let's recall some times when a friend treated you with the same kindness shown by the four men to their paralytic friend. Perhaps a good friend called you higher when you were making choices that did not reflect your values. Perhaps a good friend initiated a difficult conversation about your choice to have premarital sex with

your boyfriend, knowing it was leading you away from Christ and wanting better for you. Perhaps a good friend helped you through a time of great distress in your family. Perhaps a good friend inspired you by her example of holiness to strive for your own. Perhaps a good friend simply sat with you and listened as you sobbed, barely able to express what you were feeling in words. We have shared so many sacred moments, sacred conversations, sacred seasons with good friends who have lived the definition of what it means to be a friend.

So often we take friendship for granted. We don't thank our friends for journeying with us in this way, or we don't consciously stop to appreciate the gift of having friends to accompany us through life.

If you are discouraged by the lack of good friends in your life, I want to share with you a lesson a couple of geese taught me some weeks ago. In my book *Go Bravely*, I talk about the way geese live and move in community. One of the most amazing things that geese do is fly in front of one another to support every goose behind them, helping one another to go farther in their journey. It's common to see many geese together, but this day recently I saw just two. And they were still flying in V formation, one diagonally behind the other to uplift it. I imagine they probably took turns leading to help one another on the journey.

I thought of how many Christian women I have spoken with who express sadness that they have only one good friend, when it seems as if everyone else has so many. These two geese I witnessed illustrate the value of quality over quantity in friendship—how, if you find one friend who is going in the same direction, and you can support one another and love one another, and perhaps have other friends join your little community along the way, that is a good and beautiful thing and something to rejoice in. To have just one friend, one support, one person to uplift and give you the strength to keep going in life—that is true gift.

You may be the woman with fifty friends at your bridal shower, going-away party, or other important event in your life. Or you may be the woman with just a few friends, and pictures of women with twelve bridesmaids standing next to them at their wedding may sting in light of the few friendships you do have (admittedly, it always did for me). But no matter the quantity, each person we share a friendship with is a gift. What is important is that we have friends who are willing to forge through the battles of life with us, holding our hands through thick and thin, up and down, difficult and easy, ugly and beautiful.

Friendship is always a gift. Those four men in the Gospel of Mark showed what it means to stop at nothing to serve and love our friends. This week, let us remember to tend to our friendships with joy and care, but most importantly with gratitude.

SOUL EXERCISE

Make a list of friends, either past or current, who you want to wholeheartedly thank God for this week. Write down some of the things you are grateful for in regard to each person on your list—what truth, goodness, and beauty they have brought to your life.

YOUR HEART'S PRAYER
THIS WEEK

Jesus, thank you for every friend you have placed in my life who has led me closer to you and walked with me in my journey of life and faith. Thank you for my friends who would break through the roof to get me to you—those friends who have not left my side, even on my messiest of days. I pray that you would enrich my friendships with your love. Awaken my heart to see the ways I can be the kind of friend who would break through a roof to bring them to you—the kind of friend who speaks truth with love and shines your light into the hearts of all. Amen.

Week 36

Say No

Are you a yes-woman? Are you someone who has a hard time saying no, even when an idea or opportunity is a less-than-stellar choice for you? I've definitely been there.

People ask me to do many different things—give talks, help out, volunteer, write for their blog, assist with videos—and I used to say yes to everything. It wasn't that I wanted to be a part of everything, or that I discerned that the Lord wanted me to say yes to all of those things—I just didn't want to let people down. I wanted to help people in every capacity possible. But then the overwhelm hit. I was saying yes to everything and doing nearly nothing with excellence or passion or true joy.

It can be difficult to say no when someone asks us to do something good. Sometimes we say yes without thinking about it when we're asked to volunteer, join a team, or give of our time, effort, and energy in some way. We don't want to disappoint or upset people by saying no. The term *people pleaser* may come to mind—we like to please everyone, so we never say no.

But do you know that Jesus said no?

In Luke 4, Jesus performs many miracles in one town. He heals Simon's mother-in-law. He heals other people, casts out demons, and does miraculous works, transforming hearts and helping many. As he prepares to move on to another place, the people ask him to stay. They do not want him to leave (quite a difference from Mark 5:17, when the people *beg* Jesus to leave because he and his miraculous works are disrupting their routine!). Surely, if he had said yes, he could have cured more people and convicted more hearts to turn toward him. But when asked to stay to do these good works, he says no. He tells them, "To the other towns also I must proclaim the good news of the kingdom of God, because for this purpose I have been sent" (Lk 4:43). Jesus shows us how to say no to a good thing so that we have room in our lives to say yes to what he really wants us to do.

It can be part of our nature as women to want to please everyone. And it's easy to say yes until we realize that overcommitting ourselves has stretched us too thin. We have to be cautious of overextending ourselves to the point where we no longer give all of ourselves in the core areas of our life—our family, our marriage, our prayer life, the place where we feel God is truly calling us to invest our hearts. Do you take the time to pray and discern before you say yes to things? Or are you the woman who everyone knows will say yes, and allow your generosity to be taken advantage of? I know many women who are caught in a difficult cycle of saying yes for many seasons, then learning to say no and feeling guilty for doing so.

Jesus gives us a great gift in Luke 4:43. He gives us the gift of peace in knowing that it is perfectly good to say no when we should, or when we have discerned that saying yes is not what God is asking of us at that time. He gives us the freedom to do as he did.

This week I invite you to reflect on how you make choices. We should feel the freedom to model Jesus' example of saying no if that is the better choice. Here are some simple steps in discerning how to make a decision.

1. Clearly identify the choice you have to make.
2. Take time to pray about the choice. Map out the pros and cons, evaluate the responsibilities you have already taken on in your life, and bring your thoughts to the Lord. Converse with him about it and really listen to his response. This may take time—be patient in prayer.
3. Discuss the choice with someone you trust—a mentor, a parent, or someone who knows you and your current season of life well.
4. Make a firm decision.
5. Trust that in taking steps 1–3, you made a good, clear, prayerful decision. Have peace and confidence in the choice you made, no matter what others may think about it.

SOUL EXERCISES

1. Are you a people pleaser, or have you been one in the past? Do you want everyone to be happy with you? Why or why not?
2. Do you struggle to say no? What can you personally learn from the example of Christ, and how can you apply it to your own life?

YOUR HEART'S PRAYER THIS WEEK

Jesus, thank you for illustrating by your life that it is okay to say no. When I am tempted to try to please everyone, guide my decision-making in your will. Give me the grace to see that I can't do everything and serve everyone, but there are specific places where you are calling me to serve and give of my time, talents, and treasure. Wash away any guilt I may feel for my prayerful choice to say no, and give me the courage to always be concerned first with pleasing you. Amen.

**Week
37**

Love Your Mom

In 2010, my mom and I sat by my grandma's bedside in the hospital during the last few days of my grandmother's life. My mom always cared for my grandma as a good and faithful daughter, but they never had an especially close bond. My mom and I, on the other hand, are very close. I call my mom nearly every day, and I consider it an enormous gift that we have such a good relationship. I always knew it was a great blessing to be close to my mom, but it didn't truly sink in until we were sitting together that day at the hospital.

My grandma was unresponsive but still alive, and I felt a powerful collision of sorrow and gratitude. I felt deeply thankful for my relationship with my mom, yet deeply sorrowful at the same time that my mom did not experience the same close relationship with her own mother. The pain I felt for my mom in that moment was piercing.

Our relationships with our mothers can be a very sensitive facet of our lives. Some of us have not seen or talked to our mothers in years. Some of us have had to distance ourselves from our mothers because of unhealthy behaviors or lifestyles, and some of our mothers have passed away. Some of you may have been adopted by your parents and have a very special relationship with your mom. Some of us may still live with our mothers and see them every day. But whether you are close or distant from your mom, one thing is true: God picked your mom specifically for you. Your mom, in turn, said yes and chose life for you. And that is reason to give thanks.

As I walked through my pregnancy with Zion, I came to see how much a woman undergoes in pregnancy and childbirth. I reflected long and hard on how every person who has ever lived had a mother who endured that experience for them for many months. Your mom went through it for you, and mine went through it for me, and this is a reality that will never change.

The first sound you ever heard was the heartbeat of your mother. Is that not astounding to consider? That you and your mom shared the closest of spaces for many months is a miraculous reality.

It may be easy for you to shout, "Thank you, Lord, for my mom!" or it may be deeply painful to try to utter those words. I write this reflection with sensitivity and compassion for wherever you stand in your relationship with your mom. But I invite you this week to reflect in gratitude on your mom's choice to bring you into this world and on all that she has taught you since the day you were born.

She who bore you is an imperfect child of God herself. And you are breathing right now because she said yes. You get to partake in the beauty of this life and do many wonderful things—make friends, sing songs, soak in sunsets, fall in love, swim in the ocean, love people, and walk along the wonderful journey of life with Christ—because your mom gave you life. What did she teach you? What is she still teaching you? And have you loved her well?

Even if you find it easy to show love to your mom, you can likely find an area or two where you can improve in loving her well. And if she is not easy to love, Christ invites you to make your best effort. This is what my mom illustrated for me by her life and care for my grandma—that even when your mom has not been the mother you may wish she had been for you, you can still love her well, in whatever way you discern God is asking, whether that is through tangible actions or in prayer.

This is a week to do some digging into how you can love your mother well and be more intentional about giving thanks for her—to search within your heart and in prayer with the Lord about actions you can take to love her more fully and ever more like Christ. Perhaps it is in your speech about her, perhaps it is in calling her more, perhaps it is in working toward the ability to thank God for her, perhaps it is in making a point to pray for her soul every day. I invite you to explore this with the Lord in prayer and reflection, that you may throughout this week and the rest of your life lift your voice and heart to say,

Lord, thank you for the gift of my mother. Thank you for the gift of her life, and her yes to giving life to me. I am forever grateful.

SOUL EXERCISES

1. Take that tangible step to love your mom this week. Whether it's going to lunch with her, changing your tone when you speak to her, or praying for her soul every day, take some time to love her intentionally.

2. Don't forget your mother in heaven: Thank God that Mary said yes to becoming the Mother of Jesus. Read the Gospel of Luke and reflect on Mary's example of motherhood, from the wedding feast at Cana to Christ's death on the Cross. Think about her love for Christ. How can you come to a greater love for her Son?

YOUR HEART'S PRAYER THIS WEEK

Jesus, thank you for the gift of my mother. Thank you for the gift of her life, and her yes to giving life to me. You know our relationship has not always been perfect, but I ask that you give me the grace to be a loving daughter from this day forward. Help me to love my mother as you loved yours. Give me the grace to love her well, whether in tangible love and service or in love through prayer. Amen.

Week
38

Love Your Dad

Nothing impacts the way we view God the Father more than our relationship with our earthly father. It is a delicate topic that can be difficult to delve into, because we all have different experiences of the range of love our fathers have or have not shown us.

Our father's love is the first experience we have of receiving love from a man. As young girls, each of us had a desire to know that we were loved, valuable, and wanted by our fathers. For some women, their fathers have fulfilled that desire, and they have been present and loving every step of their lives. For other women, their fathers were not present, even at their birth, and they were raised by their valiant and loving mothers. The desire to hear their father speak those truths was never fulfilled.

Our experience with our father, shaped throughout our lives, projects directly onto our view of God the Father. It may be that your father has been supportive, loving, kind, and present to you, and it is easy for you to see God the Father the same way. Perhaps your dad has been a pillar of strength in your life, and you talk to him often. Maybe he is loving and affectionate, and these qualities in your father have helped you to see God the Father as a close, loving God. Perhaps you knew that every time you looked into the audience as a small girl at one of your games or performances, you would find your father there with a look of pride and joy on his face.

Or maybe you could not use a single one of those words—supportive, loving, affectionate, kind—to describe your dad, so you have struggled to believe how God could be any of those things throughout your life. Perhaps you knew as a child at every single event that you would look out and your dad would not be there. Your father may have been reserved with showing his love, or even absent or abusive, and you haven't spoken with him in a very long time. Perhaps he put his work or his addictions before his love for you, and you have trouble believing that God could care about you so much. You struggle to believe that you are worthy of love at all. If this has been your experience, I tell you with sincerity that my

heart breaks for you and how this has affected you. You deserve a father who was loving and present.

I tell you this with the utmost sensitivity and tenderness: my dad is in the first group—the present, loving, good, kind fathers. There has never been a day when I have questioned my dad's love for me, whether he believes in me, whether he would do anything for me. As I have walked this road in ministering to women, it has become one of the most sensitive pains in my life to realize that every woman did not have a dad as deeply loving as mine. God has a reason for the way he created each of our families, and no one's father is perfect, but I wish with every part of my heart that every woman would have had an experience of love from her father that made it so natural to believe that, yes, God's love for her is *unconditional*, is *personal*, and is *limitless* because her father's love was exactly that. The Father wants us to know that his love is not dependent on anything except our existence. It is personal and unique to each one of us; truly, his love is for *you*. And beyond that, the love of God the Father knows no end.

We all share this deep desire to be loved by our dads, certainly—but I think even more than that, we want to be *known* by our fathers. We want our fathers to know who we are, to know what we need, to know what we are going through, to know us deeply and love us still. We have always wanted this.

And whether or not our father fulfilled this desire in our hearts, God did. And God will. Because he is a perfect Father.

He is the Father who sees all of you—all the beauty, all the mistakes, all the order, all the mess—and loves you still. He is the Father who doesn't look away, but runs toward you as the father ran to the prodigal son (Lk 15:20). He is the Father who is always on time, who always shows up, who never gives up on you.

He knows every facet of who you are and loves you still. He loves you for *you;* his love is not based on your grades, or your accomplishments, or how many points you score in a game. His

love for you is first—there is nothing before it—no work, no addictions, no money, no others. He wants you to know this, to believe this, and to cry out to him as your Father. He wants you to hear him call you by your name, to hear him call you daughter, to step into those places where your father lacked and pour out his love.

He is the Father who will never stop being good and kind. This week, ask him to help you step into belief that his goodness and kindness are for you. Because they are, and they always will be. His Fatherly heart will always be for you.

SOUL EXERCISES

1. It is vital to the health of our heart and our rela-
    tionship with the Lord to do the work to recog-
    nize how the way our earthly father treated us
    impacts our view of God. This takes careful (and
    sometimes painful) reflection and prayer. It takes
    a real, necessary look at past experiences and
    memories, examining the qualities your father
    showed you or that you wish he had shown you.
    Invite God to reveal to you how your father's love
    for you has impacted your view of him and his
    love for you.

2. If your dad is still living and present in your life,
    do something extra this week to show him love.
    Give him a call, take him out to lunch or dinner,
    or send him a card in the mail.

3. We are each called to pray for and love our
    earthly fathers however we can. Even if your
    relationship with your dad is strained or nonex-
    istent, I invite you to pray for him this week. Make
    a heartfelt prayer each day for him, offering him
    and his life to God the Father.

YOUR HEART'S PRAYER
THIS WEEK

God, I thank you and praise you for being a perfect Father. I ask you to help me remember that you love me endlessly, that you know the depths of my heart, and that I can turn to you in times of need. Father, you knew me before I entered this world and will welcome me home when I leave it; I ask that you keep guiding me closer to your Fatherly heart. Thank you for being my Father and for believing in me. Because of you, I know what it is to be known and to be loved. This is a gift beyond compare, and for that I am grateful. Amen.

Week 39

Cultivate Food Gratitude

Do you say grace before meals? If yes, do you really thank God in your heart? Is it a true prayer, or just a habit you grew up with?

During my freshman year of college, I went to the all-you-can-eat dining hall (appropriately called Pitchforks, a nod to our school mascot, the devil) for meals. I ate there morning, noon, and night. When I walked in, they swiped my student ID, and I could go to the sandwich bar, the grill, the cereal bar, or the salad bar and eat as much as I wanted. Visiting that hall for my meals was simply a routine activity for me. I never stopped to say, "Wow, this is amazing! Not only is there food for me to eat, but the options are plenty and I will not go hungry today!" I don't remember many times that I said grace consciously or thoughtfully before having a meal.

During Zion's first sleep regression, he cried at one-and-one-half-hour intervals all night long. It was a nightmare for me. One time, I was in his nursery at about three o'clock in the morning when Daniël came to support me. I burst out crying and said, "I'm already stressed thinking about what I'll cook for dinner tonight!" Cooking is the most burdensome part of homemaking for me. I am not bad at it, but the thought of having to figure out what to put on the dinner table every night for an undetermined number of years overwhelms me. But the reality is this: I have food to cook every night. For the past four years of marriage, I have had no concerns about the ability to buy food to cook, and I take this blessing for granted. I took the dining hall in college for granted. We take so much of God's provision to us through food for granted.

For so many people in the world, having three meals a day is not a given. And these people live not just in poor countries, but in our countries, our communities, our cities, even our neighborhoods. Perhaps there have been times when you have gone hungry, when bread and peanut butter were all that your family could afford, if that.

Many of us attend weddings with elaborate dinner feasts, drive through McDonald's when we feel like it, enjoy a big potluck at

school, open the fridge to see what's inside . . . but do we think about what a gift it is to have food to eat? We take for granted something so many people in the world long for—food on the table.

We also tend to forget about those who are responsible for much of the fresh food we eat—farmers. When was the last time you ate a fresh, nutritious salad and thanked God for the farmer who grew the lettuce and fixings? When was the last time you washed fresh vegetables to throw on the grill and thought of the people whose livelihood it is to grow those vegetables? The farmers who work 365 days a year to grow their crops and tend their animals provide nourishment for our bodies so that we can thrive as human beings. Let us not forget them in our prayer!

This week is about giving thanks to God for the food we eat, something that has become such a normal part of our lives that we overlook the true gift it is. When we pause to think about the gift of God's provision in food, we grow in gratitude. All of a sudden, hard days gain some perspective when we give true and sincere thanks for a hot dinner on the table. This week, pause before every meal and snack to give thanks to God for his blessings, especially nourishing food. Recall the farmers whose life's work is to grow the food you enjoy, and ask God to bless their lives. And watch how your perspective shifts when you live with this level of intentionality, even with something as simple as the food you eat.

SOUL EXERCISE

What can you do to help feed others this week?
Here are a few ideas:

- ♥ Take a meal to a new mom or a sick friend.
- ♥ Help out at the local soup kitchen or food pantry.
- ♥ Make a donation to the food bank at your church.
- ♥ Send an extra lunch with your child for a child at school who may not have one.

YOUR HEART'S PRAYER THIS WEEK

Jesus, thank you for the food on my table that I take for granted far too often. So many people in the world go hungry, and so often I overlook the gift that it is to have food to eat. Awaken my heart to gratitude for your provision on my table and nourishment for my body! Amen.

Week
40

Be Patient
with
the Present

Many people view patience as the kindly toleration of someone else. Maybe we don't show our frustration when our food order is delayed, when a student isn't grasping a concept, or when the toddler is going nuts. We tend to think about patience in terms of other people. We also might view patience as a virtue we practice as we anticipate an event: you can't wait for your wedding day, you want Christmas to arrive, your baby's due date couldn't come any sooner, and so on. But we are going to focus on another aspect of patience this week: the grace to embrace *now* instead of rushing through the present impatiently or carelessly. Christ invites us to practice patience and focus in a way that is properly ordered and intentional—as he shows us with his own life.

Jesus was the most patient person in all of history. He was perfectly patient in that he was present to every situation and every person in that moment—never looking ahead, never in a hurry.

One of the key aspects of discipleship is to become like the leader you are following—and for us, that is Jesus Christ. And so we are called to be like Christ in this way—always present and never in a hurry. Certainly, there was hustle and bustle around him, just as there is for us in our daily lives. He found himself in dense crowds and there may have been a lot of hurry around him, but he was always both patient and present.

Patient with the present moment—it's how he wants us to live.

If you read the gospels and meditate on the life of Christ, you will not see Jesus rushing around, trying to get to the next miracle. I imagine he did not look over someone's shoulder at the next person to talk to or tap his foot just waiting to get out of a conversation. I like to imagine the way he must have looked people in the eyes during his life-altering exchanges with them, totally available and unreservedly present to their every need. I think of the woman caught in adultery (Jn 8:1–11), the man born blind (Jn 9:1–6), the hemorrhaging woman (Mk 5:25–34), the woman at the well (Jn 4:4–42)—how his attention to them must have been startling,

beautiful, and patient. He allowed himself to be interrupted, and in this way was always generous, always loving, and fully rooted in his identity as the Son of God the Father. Let us strive this week to model Jesus' willingness to be present to people and patient in the moment.

Sometimes we are so focused on the next thing we have to look forward to that we miss the present moment. This is not always in the big things—the vacations and the weddings—but in the little things, too. Maybe, like me, you're always thinking about the next thing. "What do I need to do after this?" I constantly ask myself. When I am rocking Zion to sleep for his nap, I am not enjoying the moment of his sweet breathing and total relaxation and trust in his favorite place in the world. I am going item by item through my head of what I'll need to do during his naptime. And during his nap, I am rushing the whole time to get through my list before I hear him say, "Mama!" and naptime is over.

There will be times this week when you have to think ahead. Otherwise, the laundry won't get washed, or the dinner planned, or your assignments completed, or your children picked up from school. But I invite you this week to focus on what's in front of you and to stop rushing. Stop speeding on the freeway for no reason, stop doing four things at once, stop being absent from the current moment while looking at the next one.

It is time to let go of the attitude, "I can't wait until this is over so I can get to the next thing." Christ is teaching us now. He is with us now. Now is sacred and unrepeatable; it is one of the finite moments you get in your one wild and precious life. Live it with focus. Live it with patience. Live it well.

SOUL EXERCISES

1. Reflect on your ability to be present, looking at what is in front of you rather than always looking ahead. Are there changes you need to make in this area?
2. Look into the eyes of people you converse with this week. Strive to give them the same focused presence Jesus would give them.
3. Identify something you are currently looking forward to in your life. Offer Jesus your excitement about that thing, and pray that in the midst of your excitement, he would help you embrace the waiting and the present moment.

YOUR HEART'S PRAYER THIS WEEK

Jesus, I don't want to spend my life rushing or always looking toward the next thing. I want to spend my life being present to today—to the blessings you have for me and the glory you are revealing in the here and now. I want to live with a heart wide open to my life, to the people in it, to the call you have placed on my life in this moment. Help me to be patient with the present; awaken my heart to see that the present is glorious because you are here with me in it. Amen.

**Week
41**

In college I decided to do an extended fast for the first time in my life. One of my best friends, who had a sibling who was far from God, asked me, "Do you want to do a year-long fast with me as a prayer for my brother to come to know God?"

So, together, we gave up ice cream. When I was in college I really, really liked ice cream. I still do, but I ate it a lot back then during stressful nights of studying and writing papers. I knew that giving up ice cream for a year would be a challenge for me. So, we embarked on a year-long fast. Years later, I fasted from soda for six months before my wedding as a prayer for my husband-to-be. It can sound a little silly when I write it out. *You fasted from soda as a prayer for your husband?* Yes. I drank a fair amount of soda then, and I knew it would be a difficult habit for me to break and that it would remind me again and again to pray for Daniël as we prepared for marriage.

Fasting is an important element in many religions. As a Catholic, I associate fasting most closely with the liturgical season of Lent. But fasting is a spiritual tool that we can use throughout the year. In fasting outside of Lent, people usually pick an intention to fast for, whether that's for their own personal holiness, another person, or a special prayer. And it's not a deal we strike with God—"If I fast from this, you have to do this." It is a simple prayer and sacrifice we can make to God.

What fasting from ice cream and soda did for me was offer me a reminder and an opportunity to pray for my designated intention with my whole heart. Through fasting I also grew in self-discipline; it was a spiritual means of drawing closer to God by denying myself in small moments. Consciously and intentionally withholding something from myself through fasting has been important in developing the cardinal virtue of temperance (self-control, abstaining, or discretion) in my life. When I stood at the soda fountain at Chipotle in the six months before my wedding, I affirmed my

decision not to be controlled by my desires and to pray for Daniël. I allowed myself to be strengthened by this one simple sacrifice.

In scripture, Jesus himself shows us the importance of fasting. He spent forty days and nights fasting in the desert (Mt 4:1–11) as an entering into deep prayer and intimacy with God the Father. In Luke 5:33–35, Jesus even says that we will fast when he is not with us.

In our fast from ice cream, my friend and I saw our intention for her brother slowly answered over time. He began to be open to a life of faith, and we were very encouraged by the active change we saw in the midst of our prayers. But sometimes we do not see immediate results for the intention we pray for. Fasting may not change another person or have an obvious outcome, but it can always change us.

Fasting does not have to involve food or drink. I have friends who have fasted in creative ways to draw closer to God during Lent. Fasting from sleeping on a mattress, from hot showers, and from wearing shoes are a few outside-the-box choices they have made. This week you may decide to fast from taking the elevator and instead take the stairs, praying for your intention as you walk up. You may decide to fast from all drinks except water. You may choose to fast from watching TV, or from listening to the radio in the car every morning. Pick a fast that is meaningful for you this week.

In a world focused on constant consumption, this week is about denying ourselves for a greater good. It is about making a sacrifice to remind ourselves that we do not have to be controlled by our desires—that we can deny ourselves to grow in holiness—and that God alone suffices.

SOUL EXERCISES

1. Choose one thing you will fast from this week—something challenging for you. Why did you make this choice? What is your intention in making this fast?
2. Fast from that thing and offer your sacrifice to God every time you deny yourself. Do not tell other people about your fast unless it is necessary.

YOUR HEART'S PRAYER
THIS WEEK

Jesus, I ask that you bring me to greater holiness through the practice of fasting. May I learn to lean into your love rather than into my fleshly desires. Help me to offer this sacrifice to you with my whole heart and soul this week, and to come to a deeper understanding of the reality that you alone suffice. Amen.

Week 42

Give Your Mornings to God

This is the day the LORD has made;
let us rejoice in it and be glad.
—Psalm 118:24

213

When was the last time you woke up in the morning and made an honest and spirited prayer of thanksgiving to the Lord? "Lord, what a gift it is to get to live another day! Thank you for another morning, another day, another opportunity to love you!"

A few years ago, I was overwhelmed by all that was going on in my life, and I decided to make my own retreat. I shut off my phone (I was dating Daniël then and told him of my desire for retreat, which he was very supportive of) and didn't watch TV or movies. I simply took a week of quiet, working my job as usual, but spending most of my free time at church, in stillness at home, or going to museums to ponder and enjoy the art in the quiet. The most interesting part of this retreat turned out to be each morning. Instead of checking my emails or social media to begin my day, I looked at the way the light came into my room. It came through the curtains and left beautiful streaks on the blankets. Do you look at the way the light spills into your room in the morning? I would thank God for the day, and begin in prayer, just for a few minutes. This habit soaked my mornings and the beginning of my entire day in peace. How do you start your days? What is the first thing you do in the morning?

In regard to morning time, Edith Stein, also known as St. Teresa Benedicta of the Cross, once said, "Let go of your plans. The first hour of your morning belongs to God. Tackle the day's work that he charges you with, and he will give you the power to accomplish it." Although I have reflected on that quote, I have reluctantly concluded that it doesn't work for my life right now. It worked well for Edith because she was a Carmelite nun, but we laypeople who don't live in quiet convents usually have a lot going on in the morning. At the beginning of my marriage, when I was working from home, I could spend an hour in prayer in the morning. But now with my son, everything has changed. And perhaps one hour is not possible for you, either. There are classes to get to and children to dress and a time to be at work and a commute to drive!

But what if you made Edith's way of living work for your life, in the way that you can make it so, for just one week?

Most of us keep our phones by our bed at night. For many people it is the last thing they touch before they sleep and the first thing they touch when they wake up. Few of us ever turn them off. Some years ago, my friend Sarah challenged a roomful of people during a talk to put a cross next to their bed instead of their phone, to let the first thing they touch in the morning be a reminder of God's love for them and God's gift to them of a brand-new day. This week, don't let your phone be the first thing you touch. Place something else next to your bed, something that will remind you to spend the first part of your morning with God . . . even if that is just a few minutes.

Some of us will have to reframe Edith Stein's suggestion to say, *The first five minutes of my morning belong to God. I will sit here in stillness, looking at the way the light comes into my room, consciously and purposefully giving thanks to God for the gift of another day of my life.* Maybe it's ten minutes. Maybe you have one hour. Maybe you will place a cross near your bed. Perhaps it's your Bible. Maybe it's another special item that will remind you to give thanks. Give what part of your morning you can to the Lord, and let it start your day in peace. To wake up is a gift. To open our eyes again, to put our feet on the floor again, to have the breath in our lungs to say, "This is the day the Lord has made, I will rejoice and be glad!" It is all gift.

SOUL EXERCISES

1. Carve out space in your morning for God this week, however much time that may be. Stretch yourself further than you think you can in carving out that space—make an extra effort to begin your day as St. Teresa mapped out.
2. No matter what you may be facing this week, make an honest prayer each morning when you wake up, before your feet hit the floor, thanking God for giving you another day full of magnificent possibilities.

YOUR HEART'S PRAYER THIS WEEK

Jesus, waking up to a new day is a gift I overlook far too often. I am alive today, and that is a beautiful and precious thing. I rejoice on this day because it is a day you have made, and I trust in your plans for every day you will give me here on this earth. Help me to rejoice each morning, to begin my days with thanks and with time spent with you. Amen.

**Week
43**

Include the
Outcast

I don't often give talks to middle schoolers, but when I do, I focus on practical ways they can live their faith in school and at home. I want to make faith more than an idea for them—an active way they can choose to live and follow Christ. When talking about how to love like Jesus, I usually bring up the person at school that nobody talks to and everyone leaves out.

I ask, "Is there a person that comes to mind?"

Nearly all of the kids nod their head with a little look of sadness in their eyes. Some don't nod because they are that child I am describing. I stress to them the importance of including that person—whether it's at their lunch table, on their birthday invitation list, or simply in a conversation they are having at their desks before the bell rings and class begins. This problem goes far beyond middle school. Every school, every workplace, every college, every youth group, every church has people like this—people of all ages who are left out, who eat lunch alone, or who are treated differently than other people for a myriad of reasons.

It's difficult to understand how much it means to be included even in the littlest of ways unless you've known what it's like to be excluded. Some people have known this feeling for most of their lives. Years ago, at the high school where I taught, there was a young girl who didn't quite fit in with the other girls. She was never invited to sit with anyone at lunch, and nobody really talked to her or made an effort to get to know her even when she did sit with them. She struggled deeply with her lack of belonging. A number of months after I stopped teaching at the school, she sent me a message to see how I was doing. I asked her the same in return, and I will never forget her response: "I got invited to go to Jamba Juice after school tomorrow."

Another girl at the school had stepped up, realizing that maybe it would mean something to this girl to be included in the simple invitation to go out and get smoothies with a few other students

after school. If people wondered why she was inviting this girl, what did it matter?

People who are excluded often just shrink back, bowing to the opinion that nobody cares and they will never belong. This girl never begged other girls to invite her anywhere or talk to her. She never vocalized her feelings of exclusion. One of the girls at school simply had the eyes and heart to see.

Everywhere you go, there is someone who feels excluded. This week is about having the eyes to see that person, to figure out who they are if you haven't noticed, and to go out of your way to love them generously. That generous love may mean asking at lunch, "Is anybody sitting here?" and pulling up a chair next to them, or asking, "Do you want to sit with us?" It may mean inviting them to a social event on the weekend or something you are hosting at your house. It may mean inviting that woman you don't know very well to your moms' group or women's group. It may mean asking a coworker by name, as everyone sits around talking in the break room, "What do you think?" and inviting them to say something when everyone else's chatter usually keeps them silent. There are many different ways to love those who do not feel as if they belong—but we must consciously and lovingly choose to do it.

Is it not what Christ would do? Surely it is, and we are called to strive to be like him in every second of our lives—to make certain that every person we encounter knows that they are seen and loved.

SOUL EXERCISE

Include someone who is usually left out this week. Here are some suggestions for how to do so:

- ♥ Begin a conversation with them.
- ♥ Ask them for their input in a conversation with others.
- ♥ Volunteer to be their partner in a class exercise if you are in school.
- ♥ Invite them to sit with you at lunch or to a gathering you are hosting.
- ♥ Buy them lunch, or ask them what beverage they like and bring them one if you get yourself one on the way to work, school, or another event.

YOUR HEART'S PRAYER THIS WEEK

Jesus, you lived a life inclusive of everyone, most especially the outcast—those on the fringes of society who were forgotten, unloved, or left behind. Awaken my heart to who that person may be in my school, my workplace, or my family. Give me a heart to love them by showing kindness and inviting them into belonging. Amen.

**Week
44**

Choose Positivity

Have you ever shared something good going on in your life with someone—whether that's about your new boyfriend, your new job, your new marriage, your new baby, a big move—and they responded, "That's great, but just you wait! It will get hard soon! Just you wait, you're still in the honeymoon phase! Just you wait, you'll see how hard motherhood is once the newborn bubble has worn away!" I once posted photos of Zion in his early stages of saying, "Mama!" on social media, and one woman commented, "Oh, just you wait! He'll be whining it soon and you'll wish he would stop saying it!" What these responses ultimately reflect is negativity, and negativity can be difficult to be around. In these moments I want to ask, "Why not say something positive?"

My husband is astoundingly cheerful and positive. I asked him once how he remains so upbeat about life. He said to me, very matter-of-factly, "Well, positivity isn't a feeling; it's a choice. You can choose to be positive even in the worst of situations."

Positivity isn't a feeling; it's a choice.

I laughed audibly at the combination of simplicity and depth in this statement. That's it. That's the ticket. Positive people don't always *feel* positive, but they choose to *be* positive. Positive people ask themselves, "Where can I find good in this? There must be something good, and I am determined to find it! The glass isn't half-empty or half-full; it's refillable!" I am not this type of person by nature, and that is why my husband has been a wonderful fit for me since the day we met. I am challenged constantly by his daily model of positivity, because I tend to look more toward what is wrong than what is right. I have had to work for years to rewire this tendency. To reshape this tendency, I have had to pay close attention to my responses to every situation—both in my thoughts and in my words and responses to others.

Positive people are wonderful to be around; consistently negative people, on the other hand, are not. I did not want to be the person who always had the negative response, who tended toward

bringing things down—not only because that kind of person is not enjoyable to be around but because negativity is simply not Christ-like. And I want to be like Christ. So, I embarked on a conscious reshaping of my attitude. I started by thinking about the people in my life who set a beautiful example of positivity.

The greatest model of positivity I have encountered in recent years is a woman named Laura Grant, whose story went viral online when she posted a video of her husband's miraculous road to recovery. Her husband, Jon, a Navy SEAL, was in a horrific car accident that left him with a traumatic brain injury. When it became apparent that Jon faced a long road to recovery, Laura, who vowed to love him in sickness and in health, stepped up to be his caretaker, champion, and greatest supporter. Through her accounts and witness online, she shares openly about their journey together to rehabilitate Jon's brain—and she is a light and beacon of positivity like no one I have ever encountered before. She shares their trials, but she mostly communicates the beautiful things that God is doing in their journey together. Every time she posts in the midst of this great struggle they are enduring, her positivity is palpable. Her choosing to see the beauty and the good in all things is impacting the hearts of people all over the world. Laura provides a model of what it means to face the worst and choose to see the best—to choose to see where the light of Christ is shining in every situation. And positive people who try to radiate this light each day are always looking for this light.

This week, I invite you to reflect on your own commitment to being a positive rather than a negative force in the world. Do you choose to see the positive in situations even when you don't feel like being positive? How do your attitudes and speech affect those around you—do they bring others up or down?

Take time this week to think about someone in your life who looks for the good in everything and everyone. Think about how that person's example can affect your life in a constructive way. I

pray that as we try to emulate Jesus, to be his hands and feet in the world, you and I will come to mind when people think of the positive people in their lives. May we be women who share abundant positivity with the heart of each person we meet and, in doing so, share the abundant love of Jesus Christ.

   "In all circumstances give thanks, for this is the will of God for you in Christ Jesus" (1 Thes 5:18).

SOUL EXERCISES

1. Take a personal inventory—of your heart, your speech, your reactions, your attitudes. Are you generally positive or generally negative? What needs to change? What can you do to reframe negative situations as positive ones? How can you become more like those in your life who exemplify what it means to choose authentic positivity in all circumstances?

2. When situations arise this week where you want to respond negatively, pause to ask yourself, "Where can I find good in this?" and proceed from there.

YOUR HEART'S PRAYER
THIS WEEK

Jesus, it can be challenging to be positive in a world filled with negativity. Give me new eyes to see that positivity is a choice—a choice I can make each day to see the good and share it with others. Help me to show love to others by being a model of positivity and joy, a soul that looks for the good, that looks for your presence, that looks for your glory. Amen.

Week 45

Unplug

On a retreat I attended, my friend Beth gave a talk in which she described how she had implemented a "scroll-free Sabbath" in her life. She decided not to log on to social media at all on Sundays and instead devote the entire day to focusing on the Lord and the people around her. I was inspired by her talk, so I tried it—and it changed my life.

I gave a talk recently on social media and phone use in our current culture, and asked the entire room, "How many of you would honestly say that using social media, overall, makes you unhappy?" Every person in the room raised their hand, including the parish priest, who must have been in his sixties. Perhaps this isn't true for you, but it is true for most of the women I know, including myself—and true for women of all ages.

Our screens have lulled us to sleep in an unprecedented way—have caused us to grow numb to our feelings, to our present moment, and to the glory of God. Social media is making much of the world unhappy, causing teenagers and adults alike to feel jealousy, sadness, and even depression, and yet we cannot seem to stop opening those apps to check what everyone else is doing, or to take a peek at who has liked our posts, or commented, or sent us a message. Social media has done much good in connecting people (like many of you to me!), but it can take a toll on our emotional health. So, this week I ask you, is social media making you unhappy? Is it taking time away from people you love, from prayer, from things that really matter?

Ann Voskamp wrote, "Anything stealing your time is stealing your life." If you use it often, social media is eating up hours of good and beautiful time in your life—and therefore it is, truly, stealing your life. What if you stopped scrolling and chose to do something meaningful with that time instead?

You may be thinking, *Oh, that's a problem for other people, not for me*, but do you know for sure? You may try taking a break from social media and then find yourself needing to check Facebook here

and there, or unable to keep from logging off entirely. The only way to know if social media use is actually a problem in your life is to give it up for a period of time.

Many years ago, I found social media fun. I'd post any photo I took, whether it was a silly picture of my sister and me or a sunset, on Instagram. In the past, social media was fun because it gave people a way to share their lives authentically. Facebook was a place where people enjoyed connecting, rather than wasting their time fighting. Instagram was a place to post a picture and share something fun going on in our life that day, not a place to voraciously seek validation from people we don't know. But social media quickly spiraled into countless people asking themselves, "What do I need to do to get people to notice or affirm me?"

Photos of faces, some responded. Photos with blue hues, others said, since studies have shown that more people tend to press "like" on those. Then people began to place their worth in their likes and their followers, and now we are upset when we have too few likes or comments on our posts.

The Lord wants so much more for us. He wants us to enjoy connecting with others, to be inspired, to build friendships through social media—but I am confident when I say the Lord's heart breaks as we place our identity in our accounts, as we waste time scrolling instead of serving, as we become deaf to his voice in the noise of status update after status update and post after post.

So, this week is about logging off and listening in, and experiencing, and seeing. It is about taking a step back to reflect on the role social media plays in your life. God does not want you to be a slave to your phone, and he wants you to turn to *him* to find your identity, to receive comfort, to know love. Perhaps your social media use is well under control. But for many of us it isn't, and we know deep down in our hearts that it isn't. This week is about taking that step back to separate your worth from your likes, to separate your value from your followers. It is a week to look up

every moment of seven days straight to see the life that you are living rather than the life that everyone else is living, to spend time talking with your family rather than bickering with strangers in Facebook comment sections, to really, truly *live*.

And so, I invite you to take a week off from social media to see what happens. See how much more time you have, see how you feel, see how hard it is to make the break for a week. There's no reason to tell anyone you're going offline. Just take a quiet week to yourself. Invite the Lord in to help you to reflect well, to discern where you need to make changes, and to give you the courage to make those changes. With grace you can gain new eyes to see that your present day, your bouquet, the reality that you are living right now, is beautiful—because God is in it all.

Look up from your phone and see.

SOUL EXERCISES

1. How is your use of social media impacting your life and your relationships? How about your self-image?
2. Would you say you're addicted to your phone or device? At what points in your day, or under what circumstances, do you find yourself turning to your phone? Try to decipher if checking status updates and online accolades is a way for you to dodge uncomfortable feelings in your real life or just a way to relieve boredom. Or maybe both.
3. As you pause your social media accounts, how do these efforts affect your spiritual, emotional, and physical health? If you find that this pause has a positive impact on your life and relation-ships, consider making a permanent change. Pick one day of the week when you fast from unnecessary use of technology.

YOUR HEART'S PRAYER THIS WEEK

Jesus, I do not want to waste the beautiful life you have given me scrolling online. Help me to be dis-ciplined in my use of social media, to not grow deaf to your voice in the midst of all the noise. I want to

see you, I want to hear you, and I want to make sure that my use of technology does not hinder my relationship with you in any way. I am the only one who can control my use of social media, and I want to take control. Help me to be more disciplined in this area of my life so that I may love you more. Amen.

**Week
46**

Release Your
Inhibitions

I was about to give a talk to a group of young women in Texas. My friend Ben was doing a big sing-along with his guitar for all the girls, and some of them were dancing and singing loudly and having fun. There was one young girl in the front row who was going all out. She was waving her arms and doing the Charleston and having a blast. But she had a friend next to her who was trying to physically contain her from dancing. She was grabbing her friend's arms to stop their movement and pulling her back to her seat so she would stop dancing. Before I had time to go over and say, "Just let her dance, would you!" the sing-along was over, and I had to begin my presentation.

As I drove my rental car back to my hotel that night, I thought about that moment. I thought about the scene I had witnessed and how it represents so much of our lives as women. We sometimes try to quash each other's fun and celebrations (out of jealousy, or embarrassment, or insecurity), but there is often a part of us as well that tries to quash our own freedom and all-out enjoyment of things. You could call it sensibility, or shyness, or something else . . . but it holds us back from being as free as we want to be. It often stems from our fear that if we don't limit ourselves, we will either be "too much" or "not enough." We try to find the balance of being "just right" out of fear of the other two labels. I am certain that if you are a woman, you know this fear.

This fear of being "too much" or "not enough" causes us to limit ourselves in many ways. We hold back on authenticity because we are worried about what other people will think of us, or because of past experiences in being authentic when we were actually told to hold back. Maybe you were dancing with reckless abandon during a sing-along when *you* were in middle school and a friend stopped you. Or you were singing and someone told you your voice is horrible. Or you laughed loudly once as a twelve-year-old girl and someone told you your laugh was too loud so you changed it and have never *truly* laughed since. We don't sing in the car because we

don't want to look weird. We don't wear the unique dress in fear that someone will say something mean about it. We limit ourselves in many ways from living out the unrepeatable woman God made each of us to be.

I have a friend who selects very unique things to do for Lent. She has an inspiring, intimate, and beautiful relationship with Jesus, and throughout the year she applies herself diligently to a life of faith. Because many aspects of Lent are woven into her everyday life, she asks the Lord specifically what he wants her to do in Lent. A few years ago, she shared with me at the beginning of Lent that the Lord had asked her to dance, even for a few minutes, every day. And this wasn't about burning calories; it was about freedom. She was to dance every single day.

Dancing is an act of freedom, celebration, and joy. We find dancing throughout scripture—many times as a celebration of the Lord's goodness and love, an act of praise and thanksgiving. One of the most common places we see people dance is at a wedding reception, to celebrate the newly married couple with joy, song, and festivity. My friend accepted the Lord's challenge to dance for forty days, and she said the beginning was very uncomfortable. Nobody was watching her, but she felt inhibited by her own self. Dancing was an intentional, physical practice for her in finding out where she had been holding back. The Lord wanted to make her aware that she needed to stop limiting herself and be free!

Where are you limiting yourself in your life? Where are you holding your own arms down and keeping yourself from *being* yourself? This week is about throwing off the chains that have been placed on you or that you have placed on yourself and going all out in being the woman God created you to be and celebrating your life in joy. Unless we take intentional time to reflect on the ways we limit ourselves, we will never see where we are trying too hard to walk the line of "just right." God didn't create you to perpetually

try to find a balance of being "just right"; he created you to be bold, unique, beautiful you.

So, this week, sing loudly in the car or in the shower if you feel like it. Wear the unique dress or get the fun haircut. Dance like nobody is watching (especially if no one really is), and have some all-out fun in your life, whether in public or in private. You are not "too much" or "not enough"; you are a woman created to live with joy. You reflect a piece of God's glory no one else ever will. This week I challenge you to get out there and live like this is true.

SOUL EXERCISES

1. Do you remember a time when someone tried to quiet you, or in some way communicated to you that you are "too much"? Write about that memory and how it affected you.
2. Invite Jesus into this place of hurt and allow him to tell you the truth about who you were in that moment. Sit with his presence and allow this truth to heal the damage that was done to your spirit on that day or in that season.

YOUR HEART'S PRAYER
THIS WEEK

Jesus, so many parts of my heart are limited by my past experiences, by others, or by me. I deeply desire to live in the freedom you created me for. Awaken my heart to identify those places in my life where my arms are held down when I feel like dancing, those moments when I shrink back instead of stepping out, those times I have been convinced that I am "too much" or "not enough." I want to step out in the freedom of who I am, who you crafted me to be—and to live confidently in that. Amen.

Week
47

Invite Him In

One of my favorite facets of the heart of Jesus Christ is that his love is not forceful. He never pressures me to love him in return for his great love for me; he never forces his way into my life. Authentic, true love does not involve pressure.

Many women have asked me how to have a personal relationship with Jesus. One simple answer is to invite Jesus into every part of your life.

I have kept Jesus out of many areas of my life—sometimes purposefully, sometimes not. As I have grown in the spiritual life, I have come to see that the Lord never pressures me to invite him into any aspect of my life. He is not intrusive. He always waits for an invitation; this is the unchanging reality of our gentle God. But as I have grown to see this, I wonder how many times Jesus has desired to be a part of what was going on in my life but I did not make the invitation. I think of many moments of joy I could have welcomed him into, many moments of bitter sorrow during which I could have made a sincere prayer, "Jesus, I invite you into this. Reveal your heart to me in this." In all things he stands by, waiting to be invited into our hearts and into each one of our hurts, our frustrations, our conversations, the most seemingly insignificant moments of each day. We choose whether to invite him in or not. This is a part of relationship.

Jesus showed us throughout his earthly life that he loves and desires relationship with others. I am sure that he had lasting and meaningful relationships with many of his disciples, but my favorite example is his friendship with Lazarus. In John, chapter 11, when Jesus hears of the death of Lazarus, he says to his disciples, "Our friend Lazarus is asleep, but I am going to awaken him" (Jn 11:11). After Jesus arrives at the sorrowful scene with Martha and Mary, Lazarus's sisters, scripture says, "Jesus wept. So the Jews said, 'See how he loved him'" (Jn 11:35–36). These few details make clear that Jesus valued his friendship with Lazarus, enough to cause him to weep over his friend's death. That response was possible only

because Lazarus had invited Jesus to be an intimate part of his life. Jesus would not have forced his way in. We can imitate Lazarus's example and intentionally invite the very same Christ that was friends with Lazarus into our lives, too.

Think about your own friendships. When you call a friend to tell them about what is going on in your life, or ask them for advice, what you are really doing is inviting them into your life. You are inviting them into your hopes, your worries, your fears, whatever you are going through. And we can do the very same with Jesus—to be in conversation, to be in relationship, to say . . .

Jesus, I invite you into this day, into this classroom, into this doctor's appointment. I invite you into my office, into my conversations, into my fears, worries, and insecurities. I invite you into this tension I am having with my sister, my friend, my spouse, or my child. I invite you into this project, this journey of healing, this search for help. I invite you into this area of sin in my life so that I can overcome it with the help of your mercy and love.

To invite Christ into every part of your life, from the seemingly insignificant moments to the greatest battles you face, is to show him your desire for relationship with him. It brings great joy to Christ when we respond to his love, when we show him how much we trust him and want to know him, with an invitation into everything. He wants to be invited into it all—through this week and through your life. Will you invite him in?

SOUL EXERCISE

Look at what you have coming up this week, and invite the Lord into very specific areas of your schedule.

YOUR HEART'S PRAYER
THIS WEEK

Jesus, I invite you into my life. For all the places and times when I have intentionally or unintentionally kept you out of my life, forgive me. I want you to be a part of my every day—a part of every joyful moment and every difficult moment. I welcome you into every conversation, every routine task, every commute, every relationship, every meal, every morning, and every evening of this week. Be the Lord of my days and the Lord of my life. Amen.

Week 48

Let Him Comfort You

We look for comfort in many places other than God. After all, a concrete quick fix seems more effective in the moment than the intangible rod and staff we read about in Psalm 23. When we seek comfort, it is easier to pick the finite over the infinite.

When we are feeling emotional, when we get rejected in some way, when we are going through the aftermath of a breakup, when we feel lonely or sad, we tend to look for those immediate comforts. We turn to what we know as comfort foods—macaroni and cheese, pizza, fresh-baked cookies, Grandma's delicious recipes. We turn to the comfort of shopping, the comfort of scrolling or watching trashy reality TV (getting our mind off our own troubles and onto the lives of others), or the comfort of a caramel macchiato. We may even turn to the comfort of alcohol. There are many different avenues by which we try to cope with our emotions and troubles.

One of the greatest struggles of the extensive and grueling traveling I do for ministry is the loneliness I experience while out on the road. For a long time, on many trips, in order to abate this loneliness, in another hotel room all alone in a city I was totally unfamiliar with, I would browse on the Internet for hours at a time. I would scroll through Facebook, read blogs, go deep into comments sections, entering into the endless rabbit hole that the Internet can provide for anyone who wants to jump into it. And, as you can imagine, this did nothing to alleviate my feelings of loneliness. It did nothing to comfort me—it only distracted me. And in my true longing for the comfort God could have provided me in those times, the rabbit hole of the Internet was never enough.

I have found that when I seek comfort in these things, it is never enough. I am disappointed when I take the last sip of the macchiato, when the clothes I bought aren't new anymore, when the show is over, or when I've looked at every current photo on my Instagram feed. I am not *truly* satisfied or comforted; those attempts at comfort simply help me to get my mind off things or have a fleeting moment of happiness.

God does not ask us to give up things we enjoy like a special coffee or homemade cookies, but we should not depend on them as a mechanism through which we cope with our lives. We need to develop a self-awareness of why we are making certain choices. This week, let us take the time to ask, when I am looking deep into the pantry for a snack, why do I want this? When I am scrolling late into the night on my phone, what am I trying to achieve? When I am out shopping, do I really need what I am buying, or am I trying to fill some void in my life that I am currently experiencing?

One of the titles and descriptions of the Holy Spirit is "Comforter." The third person of the Trinity, the Holy Spirit, is an ever-present comfort. While Jesus was still with his apostles, he said to them, "I have told you this while I am with you. The Advocate, the holy Spirit that the Father will send in my name—he will teach you everything and remind you of all that [I] told you. Peace I leave with you; my peace I give to you. Not as the world gives do I give it to you. Do not let your hearts be troubled or afraid" (Jn 14:25–27). The Holy Spirit comes down upon the apostles in Acts 2 at Pentecost, and that very same Spirit is with us, here and now, totally available to each of us to provide all the comfort our hearts long for. One of the ways the Lord has taught me to cope with my emotions and troubles, instead of running to get comfort food or picking up my phone, is to stop and say a simple prayer to call upon the Comforter, the Holy Spirit: "Come, Holy Spirit." Instead of turning to iced coffee (my most frequent choice of finite and fleeting comfort), I have had to learn to reprogram my brain and heart to turn to the Lord instead . . . to open my hands, close my eyes, and say, "Come, Holy Spirit. Comfort me now. Be with me now." When I stop to take this small but powerful step, it gives me time to think about why I am so eager to turn to the comfort of finite things, and I turn to the true comfort the Lord provides instead.

If we believe that God is who he says he is, and that he can offer us the comfort we need through prayer and the presence of the

Holy Spirit, we should make the effort to turn to the infinite rather than the finite. Another one of the most beautiful places we can find comfort is scripture. Our Bibles are full of God's promises, full of words of comfort and peace, full of reminders of his goodness and love even in the midst of the darkest of days. Instead of distracting ourselves from our emotions or uncomfortable feelings by picking up a phone, why not pick up a Bible instead? Why not immerse ourselves in the Word rather than in the distraction of content and noise? One satisfies much more deeply than the other—we have to make the conscious and intentional choice toward the lasting comfort of God rather than the fleeting comforts of the world.

Where are you seeking comfort in your life? Where are you looking for a quick fix to make your emotions or hardships disappear when God wants you to lean into them and offer them over to him?

SOUL EXERCISE

Think about the ways you look for comfort in your life. Have you overcome a tendency to seek comfort in certain ways and intentionally moved away from that behavior?

YOUR HEART'S PRAYER THIS WEEK

Jesus, I seek solace in so many other sources besides you. I crave tangible and immediate fixes and comfort. I want to rearrange my heart to desire you, and you alone. Assist me in exercising the discipline to choose you first, the infinite One above all finite things. Holy Spirit, thank you for being my Comforter, ever present to my pain and sorrow. Amen.

Week 49

Choose to Change

What if you wake up someday, and you're 65 or 75, and you never got your novel or memoir written; or you didn't go swimming in warm pools or oceans because your thighs were jiggly or you had a nice big comfortable tummy; or you were just so strung out on perfectionism and people pleasing that you forgot to have a big, juicy, creative life, of imagination and silliness and staring off into space like when you were a kid? It's going to break your heart. Don't let that happen.

—Anne Lamott

When I first read this quote, while mindlessly scrolling through Instagram and eating lunch solo at Costco, I was immediately struck in the soul. It paints a startling picture of the way so many of us women live. It is amazing to consider the things that prevent us from living full, rich, magnificent lives: jealousy, fear, insecurity, pain, apathy, laziness, bitterness. This list is long, and it enslaves. It stifles the deepest, truest parts of ourselves. It perpetually holds us back from becoming the brilliant, bold women God created us to be.

I sat with this quote and got to thinking long and hard about when I am sixty-five or seventy-five, if God gives me that many years, and I started wondering what sort of life I want to look back on. This week, I ask you to consider a challenging series of statements that I have thought about myself. Years from now when you take a good, long look back on your life, would the way you are living now, in the present season of your life, cause you to say . . .

1. I wish I had spent less time comparing myself to other women.
   or
   I am glad I spent time learning to love myself as I am.

2. I wish I had spent less time worrying about whether God was going to take care of everything.
   or
   I am glad I learned to trust the hand of the Father.

3. I wish I had spent less time crying to God and being angry with him about my relationship status.
   or
   I'm grateful I spent my time focusing on the blessings before me, trusting that God has a plan for my life. Relationship or not, marriage or not, his plan for my unique life has always been *good*.

4. I wish I had spent less time investing in and focusing on *things*.
    or
    I'm so glad I spent time investing in hearts, friendships, people, and community.

5. I wish I had spent less time wishing I had what "she" has.
    or
    I am thankful I spent time learning to love and want what I have.

6. I wish I had spent less time being jealous of other women's gifts and talents.
    or
    I'm glad I took the time to ask, "God, what are the gifts you have given me? Please help me use them well."

7. I wish I had spent less time hating my body and not taking good care of it.
    or
    I am so grateful I consciously chose to love my body and invested in taking good care of it.

8. I wish I had pushed fewer people away because of my fears and past hurts and rejections.
    or
    I am glad I let people into my heart and my life even though it was hard.

9. I wish I had spent less time living and operating out of fear.
    or
    I am glad I spent so much of my life living and operating out of *faith*.

10. I wish I had spent less time on social media, comparing my life to everyone else's.

    or

    I'm so happy I got outside and lived, embracing the unique and beautiful life God gave *me*.

Only you know how these statements apply in your own life. If you find yourself living in any of the first set of statements—jealousy ravaging your heart, self-hatred dictating your days, fear of rejection enslaving you—it will surely break your heart to look back on your life. At thirty years old, I have already spent years pushing people away because of past hurts, and it has troubled my heart deeply. Hope brings the good news that my broken heart can help me change now. I can choose to battle against my tendency to live in the first part of statement 8. It is the good news that will stand until the day we die: *We can always choose to change.*

What is holding you back from living as the woman God created you to be? What is keeping you from radiating the unique love, beauty, and joy God gave you to share with the world? Your life is happening right now. The next moment or season of your life is not more important than this one. This week my challenge for myself, and for you, is this . . .

Don't let the way you have lived break your heart. Let the way you live now bring you joy.

SOUL EXERCISES

1. Which of the statements above resonated with you the most? Write about why that one stands out to you in regard to your own life and choices.
2. If one or more of these statements indicates you really need to change, ponder it and map out some actionable steps you can take so that you do not look back in sadness on that area of your life.

YOUR HEART'S PRAYER THIS WEEK

Jesus, I don't want to look back on my life in sorrow about the ways I chose to live. I want to look back with joy, knowing that I loved you, myself, and others well. Help me to grow in faith, hope, and trust in you. Help me to take a deep look at the places I need to change and, with the help of your grace, choose to change them. Amen.

Week 50

Persist in Prayer

This week, I want to tell you the story of my jacaranda tree. When my family moved into our home, affectionately called "Wilson World," in 1998, we planted several trees on Arbor Day. We made it a family event, and many of our friends came to plant with us. We planted a young jacaranda tree in the front yard. If you have never seen one, jacaranda trees are known for their magnificent lavender-colored blooms. A few months after our Arbor Day celebration, most of our trees were growing beautifully, but the jacaranda tree did not seem to want to grow.

After a number of years, my mom told me that there was something wrong with the jacaranda, and we had to remove it and plant a tree that would be healthy and thrive. We needed shade in that particular spot, and this jacaranda was not growing enough to provide shade.

"We can't give up on the tree, Mom. Let's give it a chance," I told her. There was some part of me (not one that was based in reason, but in some sort of faith and hope) that did not want to give up on this tree.

So, we gave the tree a chance. I watered it and put a piece of garden art by it, hoping perhaps to make it happy, but nothing changed. After a long time of waiting for some sign of progress, my mom rightfully said again that we had to get rid of it. It had not grown an inch in the years since we planted it, and we needed a good tree for the yard. But deep down in my childlike faith, I knew this tree would grow. I said no again, that we could not give up on the tree. So, I kept watering it, watching it, waiting patiently, and praying that this tree would show us some sign that it wanted to live. One night it stormed so badly that the jacaranda tree was bent over, nearly lying on the ground. My dad braved the storm to go lift up the tree and stake it upright.

We gave this tree all the encouragement we could. We refused to give up. And, indeed, after what seemed like an eternity, it began to grow. Slowly but surely, after many years, it grew into a

spectacular jacaranda, with the most beautiful lavender-colored flowers that bloom every spring. I remember when we realized the tree was alive and growing. It was such a proud moment for me as a young girl—I knew we had to give this tree a fighting chance, and it had worked.

I revisit this analogy every time I grow tired of praying for a specific intention to the Lord. Have you ever prayed the same prayer for a very long time? Months, years, or even decades? I have. It is exhausting.

In these intentions and prayers we offer to the Lord again and again, we arrive at moments when we are ready to give up, to let the tree fall over, to rip it out of the ground and be done with hoping, with praying, with maintaining faith that anything will ever change. When we are ready to give up praying, it is always helpful to return to the account of the persistent widow:

> Then [Jesus] told them a parable about the necessity for them to pray always without becoming weary. He said, "There was a judge in a certain town who neither feared God nor respected any human being. And a widow in that town used to come to him and say, 'Render a just decision for me against my adversary.' For a long time, the judge was unwilling, but eventually he thought, 'While it is true that I neither fear God nor respect any human being, because this widow keeps bothering me I shall deliver a just decision for her lest she finally come and strike me.'" The Lord said, "Pay attention to what the dishonest judge says. Will not God then secure the rights of his chosen ones who call out to him day and night? Will he be slow to answer them? I tell you, he will see to it that justice is done for them speedily. But when the Son of Man comes, will he find faith on earth?" (Lk 18:1–8)

In my ministry, I speak with women who have been hoping and praying to conceive a child for three, five, even ten years. They have come to the end of their rope in praying and hoping; they don't see the point anymore. I have met women who pray for their adult children to return to their faith—women who have been praying for five, ten, fifteen years with not a glimmer of a sign that their prayers are being answered. It is difficult to persist in prayer. It is sometimes *painful* to persist in prayer.

St. Monica is a beautiful model of persistence in prayer. She was a mother who prayed for her wayward son for *eighteen years*. Thank goodness she never gave up, because her son is now known as St. Augustine, one of the most influential people in the history of the Catholic Church and an important writer and thinker for people of all faiths.

Christ tells us of the *necessity* to pray always without growing weary. My jacaranda has been a foundational analogy for me when I feel like throwing in the towel in prayer. Now, about fifteen years after that long-ago Arbor Day, I pull up to my parents' home and still see that tree. It is thriving, probably thirty feet tall, and I smile.

You may be thinking, *Yep, that thing I prayed to the Lord about for what feels like a million times . . .* why *would I pick that prayer back up again?* I have felt this way too. You try to pray for that intention again, feeling sour or discouraged or angry about it, and you want to ask the Lord, "What is the point?" It may be a prayer for a friend, a child, that teen in your ministry, that project, that dream.

And so, this week I encourage you to persist in prayer. Do not give up. Persist with great faith as though your prayer is a tree. Continue to water it, continue to fight for it. Trust in the Lord with all your heart, and pray without ceasing. He is the great gardener. The blooms will come—in his power, in his time, according to his perfect will.

SOUL EXERCISES

1. Identify an intention you have prayed for many times—one that you are growing weary of praying for or have given up altogether. Ask the Lord to give you the courage to pray with that intention once again.
2. Sit with the question Jesus poses to his listeners in Luke 18:8: "But when the Son of Man comes, will he find faith on earth?" Imagine Jesus asking you that question and how you would respond to him about where your own faith is.

YOUR HEART'S PRAYER THIS WEEK

Jesus, I love you, but sometimes I struggle to understand your ways and your timing. At times, I struggle to believe that you are listening. Give me greater faith in your will, greater faith that you are listening to me, and deeper trust in your plan for the world, for my life, and for the lives of the people I love. Amen.

Week 51

Get Outside

Let the heavens be glad and
the earth rejoice; let the sea and
what fills it resound; let the plains
be joyful and all that is in them. Then
let all the trees of the forest rejoice.
—Psalm 96:11–12

What is your favorite season? Autumn is mine, and not because I like all things pumpkin-flavored, love wearing slippers around the house, and enjoy seeing harvest decorations everywhere. Autumn is my favorite season because of the way nature so triumphantly declares its arrival. Few things capture the glory of God in nature quite like a hillside full of fall trees that have turned every shade of red, orange, and yellow. When the scent of fall begins to fill the air, I want to breathe it in deeply and keep it forever. I don't know what it is like where you live, but in California, there is no other season that has such a distinct fragrance and feel in the air.

The tragic, life-altering COVID-19 pandemic of 2020 brought the cancellations of thousands, if not tens of thousands, of events. Everything seemed to be canceled, from graduations to birthday parties to conventions to concerts and sporting events. One mom who told her young son about the cancellations shared his reply online: "Well, the good news is that nature is never canceled, Mom."

What a profound reality expressed from the heart of a child: Nature is never canceled. Nature always goes on, declaring the glory of God without missing a beat. The sun rises and sets, the waves continuously roll in, summer follows spring and winter follows autumn. Scripture speaks again and again of God's creation singing his glory, and nature provides such a powerful experience of God. The autumn trees on the hillside proclaim his glory, a fresh snowfall rejoices in his goodness, the crashing waves of the ocean roar of his power.

Taken up in the hustle and bustle of life—in our homes, in our offices, in our classrooms, in our cars—we often neglect to get outside and enter into the beauty of nature. It is so important in the midst of our hectic lives to get outside and experience the splendor of God in nature.

Often when I think of experiencing nature, I think of my friends who are passionate about the outdoors, who love going on hikes and camping and really living the "nature" thing. I loathe

hiking and don't enjoy packing for camping trips, but in the last year and a half, Zion has taught me that you can get out and revel in nature without putting on hiking boots or making a big trip. Every evening we take a walk together, and during this walk he always finds the rising moon. So, we pause, and we look up at the moon with joy for a while. We find the glory of God in nature, even just for a moment every day.

I invite you this week to intentionally step outside and open your eyes to see God in the nature around you—even for a brief time every day.

In Dutch there is an expression that you go outside to get a "fresh nose." In English, we call it "fresh air." But whatever you may call it, stepping outside and paying attention to nature can offer us a fresh outlook, a fresh perspective, a fresh dose of positivity. Nature carries on no matter what we are going through. When we are happy, nature can enhance our joy. When we are sad, a good walk to listen to the birds and feel the breeze on our skin can make us feel better. Step into nature every day this week, entering into its ceaseless praise of God the Creator.

"Yes, in joy you shall go forth, in peace you shall be brought home; mountains and hills shall break out in song before you, all trees of the field shall clap their hands" (Is 55:12).

SOUL EXERCISES

1. Remember a time when you experienced God very clearly in nature, and write about it. What about that moment helped you to experience him or see his heart more clearly?
2. As you step outside at least once every day this week, intentionally look to see where God is revealing himself to you in the nature that surrounds you.

YOUR HEART'S PRAYER
THIS WEEK

Jesus, how wonderful are your works! What a blessing it is to experience the work of your hands with my eyes, ears, nose, hands, and heart. Help me grow closer to you as I look for you in the wonder of nature this week, as I strive to see your heart in every sunset, every tree, every breeze that hits my skin. May I join with all of creation in singing your majesty this week. Amen.

Week 52

Awaken Your Heart

It is the last week on your journey through this devotional. I pray you have been inspired, encouraged, challenged, and awakened to the splendor of God at work in your life, whether you are new to a life of faith or have been on a faith journey for many years. During this last week, I invite you to a review of your journey through each of the reflections of the past year. I am certain you have had some highs and lows, some areas where you have been stretched in your faith, some moments or exchanges with people that you will not soon forget. As I invited you to pay attention to what God is doing in your life in the introduction to this devotional, I now invite you to take a close look at all that God has done throughout this time.

SOUL EXERCISE

Take an inventory of this past year. Look back on each week (what you wrote in your journal, if you kept one) and reflect on the most impactful moments.

- ♥ Which was your favorite week, and why?
- ♥ Which was the hardest or most challenging week for you, and why?
- ♥ How have you seen your relationship with God grow and change throughout the course of this journey?
- ♥ In what ways do you see God more clearly working and moving in your life since embarking on Week 1?
- ♥ What have you learned about yourself?
- ♥ How, over the course of this year, has God awakened your heart to love more generously, live more intentionally, and serve him more fully?

YOUR HEART'S PRAYER THIS WEEK

Jesus, thank you for awakening my heart to see you, to know you, and to love you more fully this

year. Thank you for awakening my heart to trust more completely in you. I give you thanks and praise for this journey of faith, for walking with me in my sorrows and my joys, in my challenges and my triumphs. Thank you for your tenderness on this journey, your constant care and attention to my efforts to draw closer to you. May my whole life be an awakening to your glory, leading me to the day when I stand in the majesty and light of your face, in the moment when you bring me home to you at last. You are, and always will be, more than enough for me. Amen.

EMILY WILSON HUSSEM is an international speaker, author, and YouTuber who runs a global ministry for women. With more than 120,000 subscribers on YouTube, she reaches a worldwide audience of women with a message of faith and identity in Jesus.

The author of the bestselling and award-winning *Go Bravely* and *I Choose the Sky*, she earned a bachelor's degree in broadcast journalism from Arizona State University. Wilson Hussem lives in Southern California with her husband, Daniël, and their son, Zion.

http://emwilsonministries.com
Facebook: @emilywilsonministries
Twitter, Instagram: @emwilss
Youtube: youtube.com/emilyywilsonn

ALSO BY
EMILY WILSON HUSSEM

Go Bravely
Becoming the Woman You Were Created to Be

As a young Christian woman, do you struggle with insecurities and feel bogged down by the pressures and expectations of society? Do you find it challenging to take care of yourself and be a faithful daughter of God?

Emily Wilson Hussem used to feel the same way. In *Go Bravely*, the Catholic musician and speaker offers twenty bits of advice that will equip you to tackle your deepest concerns about relationships, self-esteem, and dating while strengthening your faith at the same time.

"A beautiful adventure into the heart of what it means to live as a vibrant and joyful young woman."
—Sr. Miriam James Heidland, S.O.L.T.
Author of *Loved As I Am*

"*Go Bravely* is the most honest, practical, and encouraging book a young woman could read (and should read) today."
—Leah Darrow
International speaker and author of *The Other Side of Beauty*